From a different viewpoint

The lives and experiences of visually impaired people

Sally French and John Swain

Contents

Acknowledgements

We are grateful to the many people who helped us to make this book a reality. We would like to thank all those we interviewed for the openness with which they talked about their lives and shared their thoughts and ideas. Their stories and experiences contributed in a major way to this book. The people we interviewed are: the pupils of Exhall Grange Special School in Coventry; the pupils of Gosforth High School in Newcastle-upon-Tyne; other visually impaired adults and young people, many of whom gave valuable feedback on an early draft of the book.

Our thanks are also extended to Joan McGill, a teacher at Exhall Grange School and Mr Bateman a teacher at Gosforth High School for their help in organising the interviews.

We would like to thank the many overseas organisations who found the time to write to us and share their experience and knowledge. They made a very valuable contribution to this book. These organisations are: All India Federation of the Blind; Ethiopia National Association of the Blind; National Union of the Blind of Zaire; Polish Association of the Blind; South African National Council of the Blind; Spanish National Organisation of the Blind; Tanzania Society for the Blind.

Our thanks are also extended to Tamsin Swain and Arthur Laing, two young people who read an early draft of the book and gave us their constructive comments and encouragement, and to Jo Laing whose experience as an English teacher was invaluable when editing the text.

Finally we would like to thank the *National Educational Services* of the *Royal National Institute for the Blind* who gave us their help, support and encouragement.

Sally French and John Swain

Sally French is a Senior Lecturer in the Department of Health Studies at Brunel University, Isleworth.

John Swain is a reader in Disability Studies in the Faculty of Health, Social Work and Education at the University of Northumbria, Newcastle-upon-Tyne.

Photograph acknowledgements: p9 'My Wife and My Mother-in-Law' Mary Evans picture library; p13 'The Blind Girl', 1856 by Millais, Sir John Everett (1829-96) Birmingham City Museums and Art Gallery/Bridgeman Art Library, London; p13 'Parable of the Blind' 1568 by Brueghel, Pieter the Elder (c1515-69) Museo e Gallerie Nazionali di Capodimonte, Naples/Bridgeman Art Library, London; p15 Eye to Eye, RNIB, London; p25 Garry Fry; p65 Gary Sargeant; p65 'After Blenheim' Jennifer Maskell Packer; p38, 39, 58 and 69 Sally Lancaster.

To the reader

What this book is about

This book is about what it means to be visually impaired. It is not about how the eye works or about medical conditions that affect people's eyesight. It is about the lives and experiences of people who are visually impaired: in schools, jobs, families and so on. It is about what it is like to be visually impaired in a world where most people are fully sighted. But it is not just about how the lives and experiences of visually impaired people are different from those of sighted people. Just as there are differences among sighted people, depending for instance on whether they are young or old, male or female, black or white and where they live in the world, there are many differences among people who are visually impaired.

One of the things we shall ask you to think about is the words that we use to refer to people. Names matter. We are using the expression 'visually impaired', rather than 'blind' or 'partially sighted', for instance as it is the most commonly used term. To be more precise, it is the most commonly used term in Britain in 1997, as different terms are used in different countries and the terms used also change over the years. So, this book is about the lives and experiences of visually impaired people, that is, people with very limited or no sight.

How we wrote this book

We believe that to find out what it means to be visually impaired you have to listen to visually impaired people. We talked to lots of people, including young people who go to different types of schools, and adults, some of whom were visually impaired when they were born and some who became visually impaired later in their lives. Also, Sally French is herself visually impaired and has used her own experiences to help write this book.

How to read this book

It might seem strange that we are telling you how to read, but it is important. This is a workbook with ideas for you to think and talk about, and suggestions which may assist you in finding out more. To help you we have included some **Activities**. Each **Activity** has three different parts:

Questions

We have set questions to help you think and talk about the ideas in this book. Do not think of these as questions for which you have to find the right answers. They can help you to explore different views, different ideas and different feelings, particularly if you are working with others to tackle the questions.

Things to do

These are suggestions for things you can do to help you in thinking about the questions.

Hints

These are ideas to help you in your thinking.

A note to teachers

This has been designed as an information and workbook with activities for 11-16 year-olds. Sufficient information has been provided to allow young people to undertake the activities working on their own, though small groups would be the ideal. We have attempted to allow plenty of scope for you to include the activities in topic work within broader fields of study, such as disability or 'individual differences'. We have also written the book and planned the activities so that they are relevant both to sighted and visually impaired young people, including sighted young people who have had no personal contact with visually impaired people.

As a topic, the most obvious area for its inclusion in the curriculum is *Personal and Social Education*. The issues addressed here, however, are touched on in many areas of the National Curriculum, including *Geography*, *History* and *English*.

One: People and sight

Look at this picture. What do you see? At first glance some people see an *old* woman and some see a *young* woman. Look again. Can you see both the young and the old woman? If you think about what you are actually looking at, however, it is not a woman at all. It is some black marks on a white piece of paper. What we see, or think we see, is really only an interpretation of patterns of light and dark.

The way we see is a highly complex business. It is not just to do with the workings of the eye. The eye is not a camera. What we see depends on us as people: the experiences we have had and our expectations of what we are going to see. For instance, have you noticed that when you buy a new pair of shoes you start to see people wearing the same type of footwear?

A young or old woman?

Sight is not just a means for making sense of the world: it also plays an important role in communication between people. If you see someone smile, what does that tell you? It could tell you a hundred things. It might tell you that the other person is happy, but it might also tell you that the other person likes you, or it might be an embarrassed smile, an unhappy smile or even an aggressive smile that says, 'I'm going to get you!' Also, we talk about and share things we have seen: a beautiful sunset; someone's hairstyle or a television programme.

So sight is part of our social world and can seem very important, particularly if you are a sighted person. It helps us to make sense of our contact with others, and to understand what is happening around us. However, visually impaired people do not just see less than other people. It is not that simple. Their ideas and knowledge about the world are based on less or no immediate information from the eyes. However, they do get information from other senses, particularly hearing and touch. Furthermore, communication between people, whether they are visually impaired or sighted, depends on them finding ways of sharing experiences and understanding things in the same way. Communication with visually impaired people can be different, but it can be just as effective.

Sighted people cannot find out what it means to be visually impaired by studying the workings of the eye or by wearing a blindfold. Sighted people can only find out about the experiences and lives of visually impaired people by listening to the people themselves. That is what this book is about: people, not eyes.

Two: What's in a name?

There are many terms to describe people who have little or no sight. Sometimes the word *blind* is used to describe them all, even those who have enough sight to read print and walk around unaided. Until recently, it was usual to divide people with little or no sight into two distinct groups: *blind* and *partially sighted*. *Blind* referred to people with no sight at all or a tiny amount, and *partially sighted* referred to those with a small but useful amount of sight. Some individuals and organisations use the term *handicapped*, but this is a term which disabled people generally dislike.

Today people with little or no sight are often said to be *visually impaired*. Visual impairment can refer to the actual problem the person has with his or her eyes. This may be due to a cataract, an accident, an infection, or a disease like glaucoma or diabetes. Visual impairment may also result from an injury or disease of the brain, because that is where visual stimuli are interpreted. Visually impaired people may have to face obstacles and attitudes which prevent them from leading full and satisfying lives. As you will see, this book is about these barriers and attitudes and the effect they have on people and their lives.

There are some advantages and some disadvantages of being labelled *blind, partially sighted, visually impaired* and so on. One advantage is that in some countries the person may be entitled to various special services or benefits to assist with school, college or work. Before this can happen, it is often necessary for the person to be assessed by a specialist eye doctor and registered as blind or partially sighted. Registration means that the person's name is placed on an official list.

A disadvantage which people face when they are labelled in this way is that others may automatically think they are incapable of work, travel, or managing alone. They may, for example, be segregated from other people in a special school or college for visually impaired people when this is unnecessary, or be made to feel very different from everybody else. Labels focus on *groups* of people rather than on people as *individuals*. The expression 'the blind', for example, gives the impression that blindness is the only important characteristic of visually impaired people. If people are labelled from a very early age they may come to think of themselves as less capable and less like other people than they really are. The words we use to describe people can, then, shape our attitudes and affect the way we think, feel and behave.

Some labels we give people with little or no sight may, on the surface, seem very positive. We may, for example, label them as brave or very gifted. Labels like these do not, however, usually depict people as they really are. People with little or no sight face specific challenges and must learn to do things in a different way, but apart from that they are just as diverse in their thoughts, feelings and behaviour as other people.

There is quite a lot of disagreement about which terms to use to refer to people with little or no sight. Some believe that *visually impaired* is a good way to describe people with limited sight, but not those with no sight at all. Sue, one of the visually impaired people we spoke to said:

'Blind is nothing else is it? It's not visually impaired. When you're dead you're not life impaired are you? You're dead.'

In this book we have decided to refer to people with no sight or a small amount of sight as *visually impaired*. We shall also sometimes use the term *totally blind* to refer to people who have no sight at all.

Activity 1: Words and pictures

Words and pictures are powerful things. They conjure up thoughts and feelings. They are particularly effective when they are labels or pictures of people. Everyone has labels they would use to describe themselves, or that are used by other people to describe them. Some labels are generally liked, such as 'cool' and 'friendly'. Some labels can be insulting and put people down, such as 'stupid' and 'ugly'. Some might be thought of as neither good nor bad, such as 'female' or 'son'. This Activity is about labels, what they mean to people and how we feel about them.

Q What labels would you use to describe yourself?

Things to do

Make a list of ten words or short phrases that you would use to describe yourself. Be as truthful as possible and include both positive and negative things. Try to describe the **real** you.

Now write the numbers one to ten on a separate sheet of paper. Choose the item from your list that is the most important to who you are and copy it as item one on your new list. Then pick the second most important item and record it as number two. Continue through your original list until you have reorganised all 10 items.

It may help to write this list with someone you trust.

Hints

When people do this exercise they mention many different things, of course. You might have included descriptive items, such as your age and whether you are male or female. You might also have mentioned significant interests, activities and personal qualities.

Q Why do people dislike being thought of as being 'handicapped'?

Things to do

Think of people who might be labelled 'handicapped'. Now make a list of words or short phrases that you would use to describe these people. Compare this list with the list of words and phrases you used to describe yourself.

Hints

The word 'handicapped' comes from the phrase 'cap in hand', which means holding out your cap and begging. It is usually associated with things which people are thought incapable of doing. The list of words usually associated with the word handicapped is very different from the list of words that people, including visually impaired people, might use to describe themselves. There is no wonder, then, that visually impaired people do not wish to be called or thought of as handicapped.

Q What do pictures say about visually impaired people?

Things to do

Look at John Everett Millais's painting entitled 'The Blind Girl' (p13) and the picture of 'The Parable of the Blind' by Pieter Brueghel (p13). Now make a list of words or short phrases that you would use to describe the young girl and the men in the pictures. Next find what you think of as a positive picture of a visually impaired person in this book, and make a list of words or short phrases to describe the visually impaired person in the picture.

Hints

Your list of words to describe the blind girl and the blind beggar is probably very similar to your list describing 'handicapped people'.

The images presented, of people to be pitied, are very much the same. We hope, however, that you found a picture in this book which conveys a very different set of ideas. There are certainly pictures of visually impaired people who do not need others to provide for them, who have a wide variety of interests, and who take part in a wide variety of activities.

The Blind Girl – John Everett Millais

The Parable of the Blind – Pieter Brueghel

Three: Individual differences

The experience of being visually impaired differs greatly from one person to another so it is unwise to treat visually impaired people in the same way, or to believe that you understand visual impairment because you have met one or two visually impaired people. Some people are born visually impaired, and do not know life in any other way, while others become visually impaired at some point in their lives, often when they are old. Some people become visually impaired gradually, while others lose their sight suddenly as the result of an accident or illness. Louise, one of the people we spoke to, became totally blind overnight when she was five years old as a result of measles. She remembers it being 'very strange and frightening'.

It is not very easy to understand what visually impaired people can see because this will depend on the type of eye condition they have, and whether or not they are used to being visually impaired. Some people are able to see print and pictures very well but may not be able to catch a ball or recognise friends in the street. Some people can see quite well in daylight but hardly at all at night, while for others this is reversed.

Visually impaired people sometimes have a restricted field of vision where they see only around the edges or through a small gap in the middle of their visual field. The visual field is the distance people can see to the front and to the sides.

The type and proportion of eye conditions vary throughout the world (see below).

Global look at visual impairment

Britain
Numbers: approximately 3 in 1000 people are visually impaired.
Main causes: macular degeneration, glaucoma, cataracts and diabetic retinopathy. Macular degeneration and cataracts are associated with old age. Glaucoma usually appears after 40.

India
Numbers: approximately 10 in 1000 people are visually impaired.
Main causes: cataracts, trachoma and glaucoma. Trachoma is an infection of the eye. It is no longer found in developed countries.

China
Numbers: approximately 6 in 1000 people are visually impaired.
Main causes: cataracts, trachoma and glaucoma.
(Source: World Health Organisation 1994)

Nearly 42 per cent of visually impaired people worldwide have cataracts, around 15 per cent have trachoma, and about 13 per cent have glaucoma. All these conditions can be treated with surgery and drugs, but in many places these treatments are not available. The majority of visually impaired people are over 60 years old.

The left photograph shows full vision, the right depicts central vision loss

The ability to see colour is another consideration. Some visually impaired people see colour quite well and use it to gather information. They may, for example, see a red blur in the distance and know it must be their friend's house. Other people have little or no colour vision so cannot use this type of information.

Some visually impaired people know they will retain the sight they have, while others face the slow deterioration of their vision or total blindness. Visual impairment can also be associated with unpleasant symptoms like pain, or another impairment like deafness, arthritis, or diabetes. Many visually impaired people, especially children, have additional impairments like deafness and learning difficulties.

For some people the amount they see changes daily, making it even more difficult for others to understand their situation. Care must be taken not to confuse visual impairment with the symptoms of illness although sometimes the two go together, for example when visual impairment is associated with AIDS.

How visually impaired people manage depends on the situation they are in and how others react. If the environment is cluttered with objects, and people avoid contact because they are frightened or do not know how to behave, then visually impaired people will manage less well than they would in a friendly, ordered environment. People also need to *learn* to be visually impaired and this takes time. They may need to learn braille, to get around safely outside, and to use specialised equipment like talking computers, although these are not readily available in many parts of the world.

A visually impaired person's society and culture, plus the reactions of others, all have a bearing on how well he or she will manage. In some countries, for example, India, many visually impaired young people have no opportunity to go to school and there is a shortage of basic equipment, like braille machines. Ayesha, one of the visually impaired people we spoke to, received no education until she was 14, when she left India and came to England. Some people may be surrounded by a loving and supportive family while others may not, and people will also differ according to their personality. These factors result in great variations in how visually impaired people perceive the world and how they manage within it.

Four: Different individuals – Chris

Chris is 14 years old and has always been blind. He lives with his mother in the north of England. Chris attends a unit for visually impaired young people which is part of an ordinary school. He mixes with the sighted pupils in most of the lessons, but cannot play games like football and rugby with them. Chris has someone from the unit to help him in class, for example, to read the work on the blackboard. He has time set aside each week to learn mobility skills so that he can get around outside by himself.

Chris went to a boarding school for visually impaired children for some years before attending his present school. He came home every weekend. He was very unhappy at the school because he wanted to mix with sighted people and did not like being separated from home. He remembers crying each Monday morning as he waited for the bus to take him back to school, but the teachers were not sympathetic; they expected him to cope.

Chris cannot get out as much as he would like to because of poor public transport. He wishes that the stops on buses and trains could be announced. Chris's school is quite a distance from his home, so it is not very easy to visit the friends he has made there outside school hours. Chris enjoys listening to the radio and making tape recordings. When he leaves school he wants to study modern languages and become a college teacher.

Five: Different times; different places

What was it like to be visually impaired in Jerusalem at the time of Jesus, for instance, or in Germany when the Nazi Party was in power before and during the Second World War? When we look historically and cross-culturally at the lives of people at different times in history and in different places around the world, we find that life for people is very different depending on the society in which they live. Similarly, what it means to be visually impaired differs at different times and in different places.

During some periods in history and in some cultures, visually impaired people were highly regarded and had a high status as, for instance, singers, philosophers, prophets and politicians. In ancient Greece it was generally believed that a person must be totally blind to be a poet.

However, the history of the treatment of most visually impaired people is a history of oppression. From ancient times visually impaired people, like other disabled people, have been the focus of fear and rejection. There have been many negative images and forms of oppression that visually impaired people have had to face.

As burdens to society

Visually impaired people have been looked on as practically useless; as people to be fed and sometimes even left to perish. In Europe in the Middle Ages, for instance, many visually impaired people had to beg to survive. In some countries it is still happening. In Ethiopia, for instance, a large number of visually impaired people are forced to move to urban areas and earn their living by begging. The original meaning of the word 'handicapped', as we have seen, was 'cap in hand'. Most people can hardly imagine the horror of having to beg to survive.

Visual impairment in poetry

Dante (1265-1321) wrote of the plight of visually impaired people:
'Thus do the blind, in want of livelihood,
Stand in the doors of churches asking alms,
And one upon another leans his head,
So that in others pity soon may rise,
Not only at the aspect, which no less implores,
And as unto the blind the sun comes not,
So to the shades of whom just now I spake,
Heaven's light will not be bounteous of itself;'
(*The Divine Comedy*, Purgatorio, Canto XIII: 60-69)

As evil doers

In many religions and cultures visual impairment has been seen as a punishment from God for some evil or sin the individual, or his or her ancestors, had done. Indeed, blinding was a punishment which was widely practised in ancient times. Blindness can also be used to symbolise Godlessness, as shown in Brueghel's picture 'The Parable of the Blind'.

As objects of pity

Seen as pitiful, visually impaired people have often been separated from and discriminated against by the rest of society. The image of being pitiful is closely associated with charity. Money from a church charity, for example, was used by Louis IX to build a hospital, called Quinze-Vingts, for visually impaired people in Paris. It still exists today.

As you may have noticed, these views of visually impaired people are often to be found in the images of visual impairment in the visual arts and in literature. The girl in John Everett Millais's painting of 'The Blind Girl' wears a notice round her neck which reads 'Pity the blind' (see p13). Another example is Blind Pew, the evil character in 'Treasure Island' by Robert Louis Stevenson, who hands out the 'black spot' to people who are to be killed.

Disabled people can feel that they are objects of pity when they receive charity. 'Charity' refers to money or goods which are given to people, usually those who are disabled or disadvantaged in some way, as well as the organisations that offer these services. Charities for visually impaired people, for example, run schools and colleges, rehabilitation centres, leisure activities and guide dog training.

People who work for these charities read printed matter onto audiotape and transcribe it into braille, carry out research, and run courses to educate people about visual impairment. Charities also work with state agencies and press for parliamentary reform. Many of the services they provide are of a high quality.

In view of all that charities do, it may surprise you to know that some disabled people feel uneasy about receiving services from them. They believe that it is their right to receive services, such as schooling, in the same way as non-disabled people, and that they should not have to rely on voluntary contributions from others. Disabled people have also objected to the ways in which the money is raised which is sometimes very patronising, implying that disabled people are unable to think for themselves. Negative images are still part of modern stereotypes of visually impaired people.

Activity 2: Questions of charity

We are all involved with charities in some way. This book, for instance, is published by the Royal National Institute for the Blind (RNIB), which is a charity. Some of the money from the National Lottery in Britain goes to charities. There are many ways to give or raise money for charity, ranging from putting money in a collection box to participating in a sponsored run. Some people are involved because they are employed by charity organisations. Of course, people also receive from charities in different ways, such as services or equipment. Some visually impaired people receive help and support from charities, and some give to and work for charities. Some people, however, have strong views about having to rely on charities.

Q How are you involved in charities and why?

Things to do

Make a list of all the ways you are involved with charities and then think about why you want to give or help raise money.

Hints

One thing you might have noticed in doing this exercise is that people receive a lot themselves from giving to or raising money for charity. People can feel good just if they put some change into a collecting box. Participating in events to raise money can provide hours of enjoyment.

Q What kinds of things do charities do?

Things to do

To get more information you might look for leaflets or ask at the library, or write to a charity. You will find some useful addresses at the back of this book.

Hints

As you will have found if you managed to acquire any of its leaflets, RNIB offers a very wide range of services for visually impaired people, their families and people, such as teachers, who work with visually impaired people. These include the provision of equipment, ranging from tactile maps to toys which make sounds, tape and braille facilities, and information on the availability of books, magazines and leaflets in print, braille and on tape. RNIB provides a wide range of educational services, as well as training, advice and support.

Q How do charities advertise and try to persuade people to give money?

Things to do

Design an advertisement which asks people to give money to a charity for visually impaired people. As you plan your advert, think about any questions that arise.

You might also collect as many charity advertisements as you can from newspapers, magazines and leaflets. Look carefully at these adverts, and think about what they tell you about visually impaired or disabled people generally. Make a list of the words that you would associate with visually impaired people as they appear in adverts for charity.

Hints

Though some adverts are better than others, the response that is generally being sought is pity. People might give money to charity if they feel people need help, if they feel sorry for people and if they feel that people cannot help themselves.

Q Why do you think some visually impaired people do not like charities?

Things to do

Give two reasons why visually impaired people might not like charities.

Hints

Charities provide good services for people and support them. People are not ungrateful, but they feel that there are important things to consider. Your list might have included the following:

❑ The images used to persuade people to give money can create the wrong impression about visually impaired people.

❑ The services and support provided by charity should be provided by the state with money from taxes, as most schools are, for instance.

Six: Towards a social model of visual impairment

The dominant view, at least in Western societies, of visual impairment is what is called *the individual model*, often in the form of *the medical model*. This way of understanding visual impairment starts from the assumption that it is something wrong with the person, an 'abnormality'. The disability label is attached to the person because he or she does not look or function 'normally'. The individual is seen as *un*-able, *dis*-eased, *in*-valid. The concentration all the time is on what is thought to be the tragedy of visual impairment and on what the person cannot do or is expected not to be able to do. The role of the visually impaired person is to be cured, or if he or she cannot be cured then cared for or helped to be as 'normal' as possible. The problems of disability are all seen to stem from the individual person.

In the last twenty years or so an alternative way of understanding disability has been put forward: the social model. So why is this social model of disability so important? It is important because it has been put forward by disabled people themselves,

Do visually impaired people have difficulties shopping because they are incapable of shopping, or because the environment is built for sighted people?

including visually impaired people. Previously, views about disability had all come from non-disabled people. As the Disabled People's Movement has grown (see p61-63) and disabled people have joined together in many different parts of the world they have developed and put forward their own views about the meaning of disability.

So what does the social model say? An example will help to explain. Many of the large new shopping complexes have open spaces and wide malls for people to walk along. These often have seats for shoppers to rest, large waste-bins for shoppers to deposit their rubbish and even large concrete flowerpots for plants to make the shopping environment more pleasant. However, for visually impaired people this can be an extremely difficult environment to walk around. There are no walls to follow with a white cane and their way is littered with all these barriers which help to make the shopping more enjoyable for sighted people. Why does a visually impaired person have difficulty shopping in such centres? An individual model way of thinking would say that it is because the person has an impairment. The person is incapable. The person has to change or be helped in some way, for instance by having someone to guide him or her around the centre. A social model way of thinking would say that it is the way that this environment has been designed that prevents visually impaired people shopping here. Visual impairment does not mean there is something wrong with the person, it is all the barriers and restrictions that visually impaired people face that prevent them from leading a full life. *They* are not helpless: it is *the environment* that makes them depend on others.

This then is the crux of the social model of visual impairment. People are disabled by barriers. These include not only physical barriers, such as those concrete plant-pots, but also the attitudes of others, such as the belief that visually impaired people cannot do their own shopping. Shopping precincts have made shopping easier for many people: families with small children; people in wheelchairs; and some visually impaired people with useful sight who find the precincts easier to get around than the streets because they are removed from busy roads that can be difficult and hazardous to cross. However, building an environment which makes life easier for some people should not make it harder for others. In the social model of disability, disabled people are saying that they want the same rights as everyone else, to have control over their own lives and to be able to make choices, such as where they do their shopping: a world for all, not just for some.

Seven: Different individuals – Stephanie

Stephanie is 14 and lives in the south of England with her parents, older sister and younger brother. She has been visually impaired since she was a baby and her mother is totally blind. Stephanie has undergone a great deal of medical treatment on her eyes and now has one artificial eye, and is partially sighted in the other eye.

When Stephanie was five she went to an infant school for visually impaired children but since she was seven she has been to mainstream school. There is only one other visually impaired person in Stephanie's school at the moment and he is in a different form. Stephanie manages well in school, she is in the top stream and gets high marks in her examinations. It takes her a lot longer to do the work though. She has a classroom assistant for 15 hours a week to help her with tasks she cannot do, like reading from the blackboard.

Stephanie is a very talented musician. She plays the piano, flute and recorder, and has passed advanced examinations in all of these. She has her music enlarged to help her see it, and uses two music stands so she does not need to turn the pages so often. Stephanie also enjoys ballet, modern and tap dancing and is a very strong swimmer.

Last year Stephanie went on holiday to France with her school which she really enjoyed. She also went on holiday with other visually impaired young people who go to different mainstream schools. She took part in many activities which were new to her, including dry-slope skiing, archery, bowling and trampolining. Stephanie enjoyed being with the other visually impaired young people and realised she was not the only person with a visual impairment. It made her feel more confident when she went back to school and determined always to do her best.

When Stephanie leaves school she wants to work with young children, perhaps in a nursery school. She gets on very well with young children and enjoys spending time with her brother who is six years younger. She has helped teach him how to read and write.

Stephanie sometimes feels that fully sighted people do not understand what she can and cannot do, and that they do not give her the help she needs. She also finds it difficult to ask for help especially of her friends. Stephanie often has to explain to her teachers what she needs and why she cannot work in exactly the same way as other pupils. Some people are very helpful but she wishes people would listen more and try to understand.

Eight: Attitudes of others

Negative attitudes and different forms of prejudice are key difficulties that are faced by visually impaired people. A prejudice is a pre-judgement: thoughts about, feelings towards and treatment of another person based on predetermined, fixed beliefs. For instance, a belief that 'all teenagers are rude and lazy' is a prejudice against teenagers. A person who thinks like this expects teenagers to be rude and lazy and may well treat them as if they were rude and lazy. Visually impaired people face many such prejudices based on other people's beliefs about visual impairment. It means that they are not treated as individuals in their own right, or as people to be valued, respected and listened to. Prejudice leads to discrimination and the denial of opportunities and choices.

Sometimes the prejudice is obvious and the mistreatment of visually impaired people is blatant. For instance, visually impaired people are sometimes bullied, mocked and subjected to insults. Chris told us that when he was on holiday and finding his way around a caravan site a group of sighted young men were shouting, 'Are you blind?', mocking him. Chris, by the way, answered back, 'Yes. What's it to you?'

To understand the negative attitudes that visually impaired people encounter you must not think that they only come from rude and ignorant people. Sometimes it is simply thoughtlessness, as when a sighted person does not give someone with a white cane space to pass. People who are trying to be helpful can have negative attitudes. Young people who are visually impaired can find themselves overprotected and treated like little children. This form of negative attitude is sometimes said to be patronising. We have also heard it called the 'does-he-take-sugar?' syndrome. This refers particularly to visually impaired people being treated as if they do not know their own minds and cannot speak up for themselves. So, for example, the parent of a visually impaired teenager is asked whether she or he takes sugar, rather than the young person being asked directly. This sort of treatment is not simply frustrating for visually impaired people, it is what it commonly known as a 'put down'. The message to the visually impaired person is, 'You are not worth listening to.'

Disabling attitudes

B. Venkatesh, or Venky, the Director of Action on Disability and Development (ADD) India has been visually impaired since his teens. He says: 'It is attitudes which disable. These attitudes disable to the extent that disabled people do not have self-worth, they lack confidence, they believe that they are good for nothing, and therefore they become consumers rather than contributors to society.' P. Coleridge (1993) *Disability, Liberation and Development* (p 16), Oxfam; UK and Ireland.

Sometimes the way help is given is based more on the prejudice of the supposed helper than the needs of the visually impaired person and is not really helpful. One example of this is when the so-called helper makes a great fuss or treats the person as if he or she is abnormal, or when the helper expects the person to behave in exactly the same way as everyone else. Again the message that is put across to visually impaired people is that sighted people believe that they know better than visually impaired people themselves what they want or need. Sometimes people fail to give help because they do not have enough information. One of Stephanie's teachers complained about some diagrams she had produced because he did not realise she was visually impaired. When he was told he was very helpful.

Nine: Personal responses

Visually impaired people have their own personal responses to disability, of course: their own understanding of what it means to be visually impaired; their feelings about it; and their ways of coping with the barriers they face. Having read about 'Individual Differences' (p14), you will not be surprised to learn that people differ greatly in such personal responses. Also, for all of us, how we think and feel about ourselves depends a lot on how we are treated by others. It is not easy to feel nice about yourself, for example, if you find yourself rejected or treated as if you are abnormal by other people. The negative attitudes that visually impaired people can face include sighted people's ideas and assumptions about the personal responses of visually impaired people. Sighted people can mistakenly assume, for instance, that visually impaired people are unhappy all the time and want to have perfect vision.

Look at the two photos. You may well have presumed that the photograph of the

Which photograph shows a blind person? Sighted people sometimes only see the white cane and not the person

person carrying the white cane is totally blind, while the person without a cane is not. This is a presumption. Nearly all totally blind people carry a white cane, but most people who use a white cane are not totally blind, that is they do have a small amount of sight. Furthermore many people who are visually impaired do not use a white cane. Such presumptions, then, are the starting point for the negative attitudes of others, who are concerned with visual impairment rather than the person as a person. It is because of this that visually impaired people wonder whether other people know they are disabled. Some of the people we talked to told us things like: 'You've got to keep it quiet;' 'A guide dog gives the message that you are blind;' 'There is a tendency for people who are partially sighted to try to hide it;' and 'I wanted to appear to be ordinary.' Visually impaired people have these feelings partly because some sighted people can be prejudiced and 'see' only the white cane or guide dog and not the person. It is also because people generally, and young people in particular, do not like to feel conspicuous or look different.

One of the main things that determine the personal responses of visually impaired people therefore is how they are treated by others. People can feel rejected, patronised or overprotected when they are separated and treated as if they are incapable and abnormal. Visually impaired people do not want to be stereotyped. Sometimes decisions about how to cope can be difficult. Mike, a visually impaired man we spoke to, told us, 'I use a white cane. That's more to allow other people to know I am visually impaired.' He found the decision to use a white cane difficult because he only needs it sometimes, such as when crossing a road. He does not want to stop and explain to

Disabling attitudes

John Hull was born in Australia and later moved to England and became a professor at a university. He became totally blind when he was in his late forties and wrote a wonderful book recounting his experiences, feelings and ways of coping with loss of sight. He writes, 'Increasingly, I do not see myself so much as a visually impaired person, which would define me with reference to sighted people and as lacking something, but simply as a whole-body-seer. A visually impaired person is simply someone in whom the specialist function of sight is now devolved upon the whole body, and no longer specialised in a particular organ. Being a whole-body-seer is to be in one of the concentrated human conditions. It is a state, like the state of being young, or of being old, of being male or female, it is one of the orders of being human.' J. Hull (1990) *Touching The Rock: An Experience of Blindness* (p 164), Arrow Books; London.

Venkatesh (Venky) is the Director of Action on Disability and Development (ADD) in India. He says, 'Because being disabled is nothing wrong; there is no value on it. If anything, the human value of being yourself can increase immensely, because of the sensitivity to yourself that can develop.' P. Coleridge (1993) *Disability, Liberation and Development* (p 14), Oxfam; UK and Ireland.

everyone, but equally he does not want people to think he is a fraud who uses a cane when he does not need to. This is because some sighted people do not understand what it is like to be visually impaired and may assume, for instance, that anyone who uses a white cane must be totally blind.

Visually impaired people even differ in the knowledge they have about their impairments. Alan, a visually impaired man we spoke to, told us, 'I assumed that I could see.' This is because people like Alan, who have been visually impaired from birth, have never experienced anything else and so have nothing to compare with their experiences of seeing. Sometimes people feel that they would like to know more about their visual impairments including, for example, about the possibility that their children will inherit the same eye condition.

Some people who become visually impaired in later life have to cope with their own negative emotional responses to loss of sight. They may have feelings of frustration, feel that there are things they can no longer do, be depressed and have a low opinion of themselves because they are visually impaired. People who have been visually impaired from birth can also have low opinions of themselves. Geoff, a visually impaired man we spoke to, for instance, told us, 'If I'd have been able to see normally I'd have probably been married at about 22. I got married at 41 and I put that down to the bad sight.'

Sighted people may assume, however, that visually impaired people have all sorts of negative feelings, such as feelings of inferiority or missing seeing things, when this is not so. Visually impaired people can have very positive views about themselves. They can value themselves and have what might be called a positive identity. A positive identity is the same for visually impaired people as it is for sighted people. Achievements like passing exams or playing a musical instrument help people to value themselves whether they are sighted or not.

Ten: Communicating with each other

When we communicate with each other the words we use are very important, but there is more to communication than words. A person may say she feels happy with a very sad look on her face, or may say she feels calm even though her fists are clenched. The ways people look and sound, and even the clothes they wear, give us important information about what they are like and how they are feeling. This is sometimes referred to as body language. Sighted people tend to take more notice of body language than words if the messages from each conflict. For instance, if someone says they are feeling all right but he or she looks very worried, you are likely to think that there is something wrong.

Visually impaired people are unable to make use of the full range of body language. They may not be able to see whether people are smiling or frowning and have to rely instead on the words that they use and the sound of their voices. Visually impaired people may also find it difficult to use body language because most of it is learned through seeing. If you had never seen someone wave or frown, for example, you would not know how to do it yourself.

When people communicate they look at each other's eyes to show friendship and interest. Visually impaired people who are unable to do this, or who cannot respond to the smiles, nods and waves of others, may appear to be rather unfriendly. As Sue said, 'Some people may think you're being a bit off-hand and don't want to be bothered with you.' This lack of communication means that visually impaired people can miss the warmth and friendship of others and can feel very isolated. Similarly, because communication is a two-way process, sighted people may find that lack of body language makes communication difficult even though they understand the reasons for it.

One important way in which visually impaired people learn about the world is through touch, but this is often discouraged. It is quite common to see 'Do not Touch' notices is shops and museums and precious items are usually placed behind glass. Many visually impaired people remember being discouraged from touching and feeling objects when they were young because it was thought to be abnormal. In this way they are deprived of an important means of learning. If visually impaired people are permitted to touch objects, however, it gives them the opportunity to learn and to share experiences with sighted people. It is, of course, impossible to feel large objects, for example buildings, in their entirety, but these can be replicated as small models for visually impaired people to feel. In many cathedrals in Britain, for example, there is a model of the building and an audiotape which describes the architecture so that visually impaired people can experience the cathedral through their sense of touch and hearing. Representations of a harbour or a park, for example, are more difficult, although tactile maps have been produced to show the layout of towns and cities.

Gioya Steinke gets a feel for Roman Sculpture at the British Museum, London

The frequency and the ways in which we are permitted to touch each other are governed by even stricter rules which vary from place to place. It is not normally viewed as acceptable, for example, for visually impaired people to feel other people's bodies in order to learn about their stature, skin texture, length of hair and so on. It is also very unlikely that visually impaired people would feel comfortable doing so. Neither is it acceptable, in all but the most intimate of relationships, for visually impaired people to make more physical contact in order to compensate for lack of eye contact, facial expression and so on.

Another problem experienced by visually impaired people is failing to recognise people. Louise told us, 'It bothers me not recognising people...I depend on people saying "hallo" to me,' and Paul, a visually impaired man we spoke to, said, 'You can't initiate anything and you can't always respond.' Visually impaired people are often dependent on others to speak to them first because they cannot see who is there. They may never get to know their neighbours, for example, because they cannot recognise them and people may not understand why. Sue told us: 'We don't recognise people at all so we are solely dependent on them speaking to us. That is part of the isolation, definitely. You don't know they're there unless they're talking, and if they're talking you don't like to interrupt.' Most totally blind people have also had the embarrassing experience of continuing to talk to someone after the person has gone.

There is no simple way of solving these problems but a lot can be done to help. When you talk to visually impaired people tell them your name unless you are sure they can see you or recognise your voice. Do not try to attract a visually impaired person's attention with smiles and waves or by shouting but come close enough to talk to the person directly, a light touch on the arm can also help. If you smile and wave at a visually impaired person and get no response, remember you are not being ignored, it simply means that your message has not been received. If you have enjoyed your time together, or if something is wrong, say so in words. Visually impaired people may not be able to tell by the look on your face or the way that you move how you are feeling.

Activity 3: It's good to talk

It is, indeed, good to talk. It is good to listen too. Talking and listening are two of the things people do when they communicate. To communicate is to share ideas, thoughts, feelings, beliefs, hopes and so on. Communication is crucial to people's lives. We learn and teach through communication; help and are helped; provide and receive information: the list of ways in which communication is important is seemingly endless. However, we all experience difficulties in communication. You can probably think of times when you have not been listened to, or when you have not been able to express your thoughts and feelings. In this Activity we shall be thinking mainly about *face-to-face* communication (rather than, for instance, writing letters). The questions are about the ways in which people communicate and any differences there might be when visually impaired people are involved.

Q How do people communicate?

Things to do

Working with a partner, tell a story without using words. It could be something that has happened to you personally, including straightforward things such as how you got to school one morning. It could also be a story you have been told, or a story from a film or television programme. The only rule to the game is that you must tell the story using actions. Your partner should remain quiet until you have finished and should then retell, as far as he or she can, your story this time using words. Take it in turns with your partner to act your stories.

Make a list of everything people do when they communicate, that is everything that sends messages to another person. It may help to think of how you and your partner told stories.

Hints

Your list could be quite long as there are lots of things we do that send messages to other people. The expressions on your face, for instance, can send messages about how you are feeling. So do gestures, such as pointing. Eye contact is another way of communicating. Looking someone in the eye can say, for instance, 'I'm listening to you.'

Q In what ways might visual impairment affect communication?

Things to do

Return to your list of the ways in which we communicate and underline or highlight those which might be difficult in communication involving visually impaired people.

Hints

The obvious ways of communicating which can be affected are those involving sight. Visually impaired people may not, for instance, see gestures or actions. There can be difficulties from both sides. Some sighted people can find it difficult if the other person does not look them in the face.

Q What are possible alternative ways of communicating with visually impaired people?

Things to do

Play the 'story game' with a partner again. This time, however, tell a story by just using words, that is without any gestures or facial expressions (like being on the phone). Again take it in turns.

Return to the ways of communicating that you underlined or highlighted and suggest alternative ways of communicating.

Hints

We return, of course, to the idea that it is good to talk. To say 'yes, I understand' conveys the same message as a nod. You probably found that it is easier to tell a story using words than just using actions. It is good to listen too. Visually impaired people can tell you if they have difficulties and what you can do to help improve communication. The main point is that communication with visually impaired people can be just as effective as communication with sighted people. It may be different, but just as good.

Eleven: Different individuals – Martha

Martha was born with cataracts on both her eyes. She had them treated with surgery when she was three years old, but was left visually impaired. Martha was born in Malaysia just after the Second World War. At that time visual impairment was not accepted very well and Martha was rejected by her parents. She spent most of her time in a boarding school for visually impaired young people and lived with an aunt in the holidays. Her aunt did not really want Martha and she was usually left behind when her cousins went on family outings.

Martha's school, which was run by British missionaries, provided her with a better education than her brothers and sisters received. They all left school and started work when they were twelve years old. When Martha reached her teens she went to a mainstream school and then to university where she studied English literature. It was very hard because she was the first visually impaired person who had studied there and she received no extra help. Martha then went to college where she trained to be a school teacher. She managed very well, but left her job after eight years. She had no special equipment to help with all the reading and found she had no time to do anything else but work.

Martha moved to London in England for a few years and worked as a braille proof reader, checking the accuracy of braille books. She did not earn as much money as she had as a teacher, but had a lot more time to enjoy herself and felt happy and relaxed. While she was in London Martha married and for the past ten years has lived happily in Australia with her husband.

Twelve: Personal Relationships

Peter is 15. He lives with his mother, father and younger brother on a fairly new housing estate on the outskirts of a city in the north of England. He is lively and outgoing, and yet has no friends living on the estate. He feels isolated. His mother explains, 'I think he does not exist as far as the children in the street are concerned.'

There are many reasons why Peter has no friends living close by: he attends a unit for visually impaired young people within a mainstream school which lies about eight miles away across the city. He has tried to join local clubs, in particular the local cub-scouts, but found that he could not join in many of the activities. He does not want to rely on his younger brother to take him out. He can use a white cane well but would find it difficult to wander around the streets in the hope of meeting a companion.

Family and friends are, of course, just as important to visually impaired people as they are to sighted people. As Peter's story shows, however, there are many barriers that can get in the way of personal relationships. Many of the other visually impaired people we talked to mentioned similar barriers, particularly when they had little opportunity to mix with sighted people.

Friendships between visually impaired people can be important in many ways. They can be friendships that last from childhood, with shared memories of school, sometimes boarding school. Louise told us, 'It's the mutual understanding without having to explain, and sharing the same sorts of experiences, the same sorts of frustrations. I think it is really important to have blind friends.' Stephanie found that having a holiday with other visually impaired young people made her more confident.

All human beings are unique and so are all families. The members of families of people who are visually impaired can experience oppression in similar ways to visually impaired individuals. The placement of young people in boarding school, for instance, affects the whole of the family and relationships between parents and their children. Some parents of visually impaired children have spoken about their personal responses and the unhappiness they have experienced. Families do differ, however. Geoff has the same eye condition as his father, his aunt, his sister and his brother. Talking about the response of his family to visual impairment he told us, 'they didn't think it was a tragedy at all.'

Jackie Cairns has written about her experiences as a totally blind mother having and bringing up a sighted child with Ian, his father, who is also totally blind (O'Keefe 1992). The daily routines with a baby, including feeding and changing his nappy, have caused some difficulties but they have been overcome. Their biggest problem has been going out as a family and Jackie writes about their attempts to get around by pulling rather than pushing the pram. Overall, like other visually impaired parents, including some of the people we spoke to, they have not found having a family as difficult as they, and others, expected. They can do things their own way and organise the home and family life to suit themselves.

Thirteen: Information

We absorb information about the world from all of our senses – sight, hearing, touch, taste and smell – but sight is considered to be the most important sense in human beings. Visually impaired people are deprived of a great deal of information or do not have direct access to it. Although visually impaired people may become very good at using their other senses to the full, this does not fully compensate for lack of sight. Neither do their remaining senses become more acute, although these senses are used more fully. Much of what we learn occurs almost automatically. You may, for example, learn how to tile a roof or plough a field simply by watching someone do it. Visually impaired people miss out on a lot of information of this type.

Visually impaired people lack access to information from many sources including books, newspapers, posters, leaflets, official documents, private correspondence, signs, and prices of items in shops. When Martha was a teacher in Malaysia one of the biggest problems she faced was not being able to read print or to see her pupils' handwriting. Many of the young visually impaired people we spoke to could not see sufficiently to read information from the blackboard in school. Chris told us: 'You hear this chalk going on the blackboard and you think "Oh no, I'm not getting this down"...some teachers are a bit obsessed with the blackboard, I think it should be taken away from them.'

Other problems the young people mentioned were lack of announcements on public transport, not being able to read bus numbers and timetables, and not being able to follow programmes on the television. We will consider some of these problems later in the book.

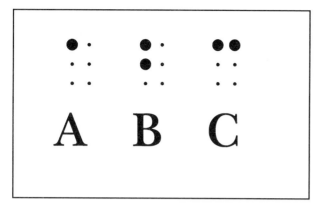 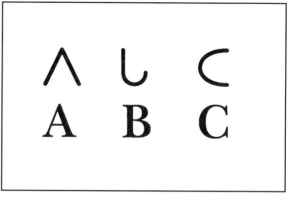

Braille (left), a tactile reading system, was invented in 1829, and Moon was devised later for those whose touch was not sensitive enough to read braille.

Paul made the important point that visually impaired people often do not know that information is there. He said 'I think half our trouble is knowing that things exist and identifying them.' The information might, for example, be on a noticeboard, but unless the person is aware of this there is no chance of asking someone else to read it. Stephanie has missed information which is put on the noticeboard in her school.

A lot can be done to reduce these problems if information is presented to visually impaired people in the appropriate format. Many visually impaired people are able to see print, but may need it enlarged or made extra dark. Some people like to listen to information on tape, while others may prefer to read braille. Many visually impaired people use a combination of methods. Visually impaired people throughout the world are constantly fighting to improve access to information.

Braille is a tactile form of writing which is read with the fingers through the sense of touch. It is named after a blind Frenchman called Louis Braille. He was born in 1810 and devised his system in 1829. Braille, which is based on just six dots in different combinations, is now used throughout the world. It can be adapted for science, mathematics and music, and can be modified for use in different languages. It has enabled many visually impaired people to read and write. Martha learned braille in her school in Malaysia; Geoff had to learn it before he could become a braille shorthand typist; Louise learned it when she became blind at the age of five; and Ayesha learned it when she started her schooling at the age of 14. It can be written by hand or with a machine and can now be produced by computer.

Braille is used by only a minority of visually impaired people, usually those who have been visually impaired since they were young. Most of these people regard it as better than audiotape or any of the modern technologies, like talking computers, which are now available in some countries. Sue said, 'At least with braille you can pick it up and read it like anyone else can read print. Braille is our print;' and Paul said, 'At least with braille you can do what a sighted person can do: you can identify information quickly and decide whether you want to read it; you can skim down it.' Braille is written as a form of shorthand because it is very bulky – a small paperback book would take three or four large volumes. Although braille can be read at a very useful speed, it is not possible to read it as fast as a sighted person reads print.

Another form of tactile reading and writing is Moon. It is named after William Moon who devised his system in 1847. William Moon, who was totally blind, was born in England in 1818. He modified and simplified raised sighted letters, which had previously been used, so they were easier to feel. There were, at this time, various other tactile reading systems for visually impaired people, but braille and Moon are the only ones that have survived. Moon is still used today by people whose sense of touch is not sensitive enough to read braille. It is not as popular as braille as it is bulkier, is less readily available, and until recently could not be written by visually impaired people. By the time of Moon's death in 1894, books in Moon were available in 476 languages.

Modern technology is now giving visually impaired people more access to information. It is, however, very expensive and is only available in some countries. Sue uses a scanner at work which reads print aloud from documents, provided the print is clear. It is also possible to produce large print and braille directly from computers, and computers now exist which talk, magnify the words on the monitor and produce braille.

Although there are many ways in which visually impaired people can gain information, very little is produced on tape, in large print, or in braille. This situation is worse in some parts of the world than in others. *The Ethiopia National Association of the Blind* reports a great lack of basic equipment including braille machines and tape recorders, and the *Tanzania Society for the Blind* explains that there is little money available for any form of equipment and most of what they have is imported from abroad. In the Beijing school for visually impaired children in China there is a

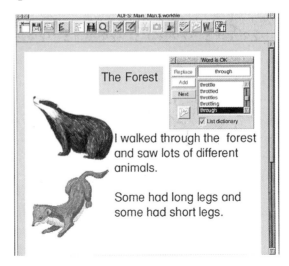

Technology can be adapted for visually impaired people. Talking computers can read out information on the screen and relay it through speakers or headphones.

Watches and clocks are adapted for visually impaired people

shortage of braille books and no money to buy basic equipment – in 1994 there were only two braille writing machines in the whole school (Chan 1994). *The National Union of the Blind of Zaire* also have a shortage of braille equipment in its schools.

There are many visual aids now available to help visually impaired people gain more information. These include powerful magnifying glasses and machines which enlarge print, and monoculars (small telescopes) which magnify distant objects like street names and door numbers.

Kirsty, a young person we spoke to, has a monocular to help her read the blackboard in class, but she finds it embarrassing to use. Stephanie likes to use hers to observe animals. Watches and clocks can now 'talk' or may contain raised dots which can be felt, and many kitchen and gardening gadgets have been adapted to assist visually impaired people, such as kitchen scales and guide wires to enable planting in straight rows. Some of this equipment is expensive and is not readily available in many countries. Schemes to export second-hand equipment, such as braille writing machines, from developed to developing countries are in operation in Britain and in other parts of the world.

Activity 4: Getting to know

It is sometimes said that we live in an 'information age'. We live in a world in which we are bombarded with information. Much is in a written form: look for instance around a supermarket at all the information on labels and packaging. The growth of technology has had a major part to play in the explosion of information, with the invention of the telephone, radio, television, computer and so on. People can now carry their radios, telephones and even computers around with them. In this Activity you are asked to think about what it might be like for visually impaired people living in an information age.

Q What are the main ways in which we receive information?

Things to do

Conduct a survey of all the different forms of information in your school. Throughout a day keep a record of the different forms of information you encounter.

Conduct a similar survey at home one evening, again making a list of all the different forms of information around the house.

Hints

There are many things you might have noted in your lists. There are many different forms of written information, for instance on the blackboard, noticeboards, leaflets, newspapers, books and labels on cans of food. There are also all the forms of technology through which people give and receive information, including the telephone and television. You might also have mentioned being told information.

Q What forms of information might be inaccessible to visually impaired people?

Things to do

Return to your lists and either mark with a highlighter pen or underline those forms of information which might not be accessible to visually impaired people.

Hints

The items on the lists that you have indicated will be those involving sight. An important point here is how much sighted people rely on visually presented information. Imagine trying to do the shopping if someone had ripped all the labels off the cans and removed all the price tags!

Q What alternatives, adaptations or support would give visually impaired people the same access to information as sighted people?

Things to do

Return to the forms of communication on your lists which you felt might be difficult for visually impaired people. Suggest ways in which the information could be made accessible to visually impaired people.

Hints

Firstly, there are improvements that can be made to the presentation of visual information. People with diabetes need information about the amount of sugar there is in the food they eat, for instance. On some labels the printing is so small that it is difficult for sighted people to read and impossible for people with diabetes who are visually impaired. Other strategies for increasing the amount of information accessible for visually impaired people involve the provision of information through alternative means, mainly through hearing or touch, including braille and Moon, audiotapes, raised maps and so on.

Fourteen: Leisure

Most people enjoy taking part in hobbies and leisure activities. People choose diverse activities to pursue and visually impaired people are no exception. The young visually impaired people we spoke to enjoyed a variety of leisure activities including football, motorbike-riding, skiing, listening to music, playing musical instruments, dancing, gardening, computing and horse-riding. Helen, for instance, had become a very proficient skier and had won many horse-riding rosettes.

Most activities and hobbies are possible for visually impaired people although some adaptations may need to be made. Adam, a young man we spoke to, explained: 'At school we have to use a ball that is full of ball-bearings so that we can play with everyone. We've got a blind goalkeeper you see so we need something that rattles.'

Horse-riding is one of the many leisure activities enjoyed by visually impaired people

Many games and pastimes have been adapted to allow visually impaired people to play with sighted people. Games such as chess, for example, have a specially adapted board where the black squares are raised, and the pieces have pegs which fit into holes, to enable visually impaired people to feel them without disturbing them. Games such as ludo, snakes and ladders, Scrabble and Monopoly are also adapted. Audio description has now been developed whereby visually impaired people receive a live commentary through headphones when they go to the theatre. This is also being considered for television. Other activities, such as mountaineering, running, sailing and tandem riding are possible with a guide or with some assistance from sighted people. Visually impaired people are also involved in acting, dance, painting and photography. Nazih Rizk, a visually impaired person who comes from Egypt, has had his work exhibited in many parts of the world.

Some visually impaired people prefer to pursue leisure activities with others with a similar disability. Geoff joined a drama club for visually impaired people where he played the leading role on four occasions.

Chess can be easily adapted for use by visually impaired people

There are many organisations and societies where visually impaired people can learn and develop specific skills and talents, for example the *Association of Blind Gardeners*, the *Association of Blind Writers* and *The Venturers* drama group in Britain.

In high level competitive sport, visually impaired people compete against each other to avoid disadvantage. Sport for disabled people is well developed in many parts of the world, and the high standards that they reach is demonstrated in the *Paralympic Games* which take place every four years. It is one of Helen's ambitions to ski in these games.

Many art galleries and museums allow visually impaired people to touch the exhibits

Art galleries and museums are increasingly allowing visually impaired people to touch the exhibits under controlled conditions and they also put on specific exhibitions for visually impaired people. There are many gardens specially designed for visually impaired people with plenty of sweet-smelling plants and interesting sounds such as running water and gravel paths underfoot. Special

The Paralympic Games

The 1992 Paralympic (which means parallel Olympic) Games had 3,500 competitors from 82 countries with huge crowds of spectators. Events for visually impaired people included athletics, tandem riding, judo and swimming.

interest holidays, for example to learn about bird song, architecture, geology, or photography also take place in some countries. In Britain a number of these holidays take place at Bristol University every year. The Royal National Institute for the Blind runs activity holidays for visually impaired young people. You may remember that Stephanie went on one of these.

Some visually impaired people become involved in activities, such as art and drama, where they put forward their own ideas about disability and their own experiences. Maria Oshodi who lives in England, for example, wrote a play called *Hound* based on her own experience of guide dog training. Most of the actors were visually impaired. We will return to the topic of disability arts in section 24.

It is unfortunate that many visually impaired people are prevented from mixing with sighted people in leisure activities. Sue told us that although she enjoys swimming she rarely goes because unless she swims very slowly she keeps bumping into people. Richard, a young man we spoke to, told us that he was made to leave a football team when his visual impairment was discovered, and Paul found there was 'no enthusiasm' when he tried to join a keep fit class. Many people said that they tried to hide their visual impairments in order to be accepted.

Most of the visually impaired people we spoke to were restricted in their leisure pursuits by other people's attitudes, poor public transport and a dangerous environment which prevented them from going out without assistance. Changes in attitude, improved public facilities, and a willingness to adapt the way things are done all need to take place before visually impaired people can be fully integrated in leisure activities, but improvements are steadily taking place.

Activity 5: At your leisure

The easiest way to think about leisure is as things you do when you are not working, including school work and household chores, as well as work for which you are paid. Leisure generally involves things we do for pleasure. There are different forms of pleasure, including relaxation, being with friends, being creative, competing and just enjoying a pastime. Here we are looking at the leisure opportunities for visually impaired people and how to adapt activities so they are more accessible.

Q What do you like to do in your leisure or spare time?

Things to do

Make a list of the kinds of things you like to do.

Hints

You might have found it difficult to mention everything. There might even have been things of which other people would disapprove. Some of the things on your list might be quite general, such as 'messing about' or 'being with my friends'. You might have found that it is not simple at times to separate 'work' from 'leisure'. We (Sally French and John Swain) both like reading, for example, in our spare time, but some of the reading we do helps us in our work. In general, the main thing is that we all like to choose what we do in our spare time. We all like to please ourselves.

Q What do people generally like doing in their spare or leisure time?

Things to do

Write down five to ten things that are not on your own list. You could ask people what they like to do or find the leisure section in the library.

Hints

There are lots of things that others do that we (Sally and John) do not choose. Neither of us would like to go bungee jumping or hang-gliding. On the other hand, we might like doing things in our spare time which you would not choose, such as listening to classical music. Again it is a matter of choice, and the more opportunities there are to do different things, then the more choice people have.

Q What activities might visually impaired people find difficult?

Things to do

Return to the list of activities you like and mark with a highlighter pen those which visually impaired people might find difficult.

Hints

Lots of leisure activities hold no difficulties at all for some visually impaired people. Some sports like tennis and football can be difficult. However, there are a number of points you might have thought about. One major point is that it is very difficult to generalise about visually impaired people. Another is that we all have difficulties with some activities. Some people, for instance, find swimming terribly difficult. Also whether visually impaired people have difficulties depends on whether the activity is made accessible. Reading print can be difficult for some visually impaired people, but there are many alternative ways of doing the same thing: the use of braille; large print books; and audio tapes of books being read.

Q What kinds of support and adaptations can make activities accessible to all visually impaired people?

Things to do

Select one or two activities you thought might be difficult for visually impaired people and suggest ways in which each could be adapted or support provided so that the difficulties would be overcome.

Hints

The vast majority of activities can be made accessible with some adaptations or support. When Helen goes skiing, for instance, she has a guide to help her down the slopes. Adaptations generally provide information through other senses, particularly hearing and touch. One important point here is that making activities accessible increases the opportunity for visually impaired people to be involved. Having choices is important for everyone.

Fifteen: Different individuals – Sally

I was born in a village in the south of England and have always been visually impaired. When I was five I went to a tiny school, deep in the countryside, with just two teachers and thirty pupils. It was not the local school, but my parents thought I would manage better there because it was small. I could not see to read the blackboard or play some of the games and sports with the other pupils, but everyone was treated as an individual, and I do not remember any major problems. The teachers ensured that I achieved the same standards as the other pupils and everyone treated me well.

When I was nine I was transferred to a boarding school for visually impaired girls about forty miles from home. It was not a surprise to me as my parents had told me from a very young age that one day I would have to go. The education was very basic and the people who looked after us were often harsh and unkind. We did most of the cleaning and weeding ourselves and every Saturday and Sunday afternoon we went for a long 'crocodile' walk in twos. We saw very little of our families and were not allowed to speak to them on the telephone, although we did receive letters. I was hardly ever unhappy though, because I made a lot of good friends who are still my friends today. I enjoyed being with other visually impaired people and feeling 'one of the crowd'. The only time I felt really sad was leaving home after a holiday, but the feelings never lasted long.

At the age of 13 I went to another special boarding school which was much further from home. It was a mixed school with 300 pupils. We lived in six separate houses and each had its own routine. We went out by ourselves to the nearby town and the teachers ran clubs and activities for us in the evenings, such as drama, country dancing and photography. The education was much better than at the other special school and many pupils went on to university. I enjoyed living with all my friends and although I went home even less I did not really mind.

When I left school I worked with disabled young people for a time and then I trained as a physiotherapist. Physiotherapy is a job that many visually impaired people do. I was trained in a college for visually impaired students in London where we had all the facilities we needed. When I qualified I worked as a physiotherapist for four years, two of which I spent in Iceland, The Faroe Islands and Canada. Working abroad was an interesting experience although my inability to speak Icelandic and Faroese was very hard as I am more dependent than sighted people on the spoken word for gathering information.

I then decided to train to become a teacher of physiotherapy and have been involved in teaching adults ever since. I find it a very interesting job, with plenty of rewards, but it is not always easy because colleges and universities do not take the needs of visually impaired employees into account. The students are always very helpful and co-operative though; they are happy to read their work out loud to me, and if they want to interrupt me in a lecture, they talk up loud instead of raising their hands. When I first meet a group of students I explain about my visual impairment and tell them what to do. This enables us to have an easy working relationship.

Work has been a very big part of my life, but recently I have tried to find more time for leisure. I have joined a large choir which rehearses every week and performs three concerts a year. I am also learning to play the piano. Over the past 10 years I have written a lot of articles and books, including this one. This is partly to do with my work but is really a hobby too. I enjoy concerts and plays, holidays in remote places, walking in the countryside, learning new things and spending time with friends. I love reading novels and am very fond of cats.

Sixteen: Out and about

It is possible for visually impaired people to get out and about relatively easily if the environment is free of hazardous obstacles. Unfortunately, this is rarely the case. For many visually impaired people, the obstacles they encounter are a major factor in preventing them from leading full and satisfying lives. Whenever visually impaired people visit friends, go out for the day, or go to school, college or work, they must cope with pavements full of parked cars, bicycles left in the way, overhanging branches, road works, holes, sacks of rubbish, shopkeepers' goods, and people riding bicycles on the pavement. In some countries, for example Thailand, shopkeepers do most of their trading on the pavement.

In addition there is more traffic nowadays and the environment has become noisier which makes it more difficult for visually impaired people to use their sense of hearing. Sometimes large signs or bollards, which are used to warn sighted people of hazards, create dangers for visually impaired people.

Martha told us about the situation in Malaysia: 'I guess the main problem is open drains which are very deep and full of rubbish. A lot of visually impaired people fall into them and some are six foot deep. The parking system is very bad, they park anywhere – it is very difficult for visually impaired people to move safely. But I went back in June and I was surprised by the progress. There were lots of bleeper crossings and they've put a mesh across some of the drains too.'

Visually impaired people use a variety of strategies and aids to help them get about outside. These include white canes, guide dogs, and the help of sighted people.

Vehicles parked on streets are hazardous obstacles

Visually impaired people with useful sight often use a symbol white cane. Its function is to indicate, to motorists for example, that the person has very limited sight. The visually impaired person may use it in difficult situations, like crossing a busy road or walking through crowds. It also attracts help from other people and makes them more careful. It may be needed at night but not during the day or vice versa, and when it is not required it can be folded up and put away.

Totally blind people or people with very limited sight may prefer to use a long white cane. A technique is learned where the cane is used to ensure that the ground immediately in front of the person is clear of obstacles. It can also be used for finding steps and kerbs. In some countries mobility training and help in managing everyday tasks, like cooking, is available to visually impaired people, although this is often very limited. In Britain only five per cent of visually impaired adults receive mobility training.

Many of the visually impaired people we spoke to were reluctant to use a white cane, even though it would have been helpful, because they felt embarrassed and wondered whether people would believe that they were visually impaired. Geoff told us, 'I wouldn't use a white stick because it showed me up as a visually impaired person. It singled me out as being different from everyone else.' Mike said, 'I found it very difficult. In the end I used it because everyone kept nagging me,' and Stephanie felt embarrassed using hers because it made her feel old.

Many visually impaired people prefer to use guide dogs to help them get around outside, although in some countries, for example Malaysia and India, dogs are considered unclean and are not used. Sue decided to get a guide dog when she found herself getting more and more tense as she tried to avoid all the obstacles outside, and Louise and Ayesha felt much more independent and capable with a guide dog than they had with a white cane. Ayesha said, 'I wouldn't be without one now. I feel blind now when I'm not with Lindy and I don't feel blind when I have her with me.' When a visually impaired person uses a guide dog, the person is always in control and must know exactly where he or she is going. The dog is trained to guide the visually impaired person around objects, to take commands, and to ignore the command 'forward' if it is dangerous to move. Guide dogs should never be distracted when they are wearing a harness. When the harness is removed they behave like any well-trained pet dog.

Even with a guide dog, getting around outside can be frightening for visually impaired people. Geoff told us he started feeling 'squeamish in the stomach' when he crossed the road with his guide dog because he could hear all the traffic moving around him.

Visually impaired people need auditory and tactile cues to help them get around safely and efficiently outside. As we discussed earlier, very flat environments and wide open spaces are extremely difficult, especially for totally blind people, as everything feels the same under foot and there is nothing to follow, such as a building or a wall, either with a white cane or through the sense of hearing. When walking past an object there are subtle changes in sounds, like your own footsteps and people talking, which aid the mobility of visually impaired people. Kerbs, steps, and traffic can be useful to

The Guide Dogs for the Blind Association

The Guide Dogs for the Blind Association breeds its own dogs. Guide dog training is available in many parts of the world, including Japan, South Africa, Israel and Canada. There are approximately 4,200 guide dog users in Britain.

visually impaired people because they provide audible and tactile cues. They can, however, be dangerous too.

A major problem for visually impaired people in many parts of the world is not being able to drive a car or ride a bicycle. Many of the young people we spoke to were concerned about this. Stephen said, 'I'm worried. I often think about it.' Being unable to drive can mean that people feel really stuck and isolated unless there is a good public transport system. Public transport is not, however, always easy to use. It can, for example, be difficult or impossible to distinguish buses from other vehicles, to find bus stops, and to read bus numbers and timetables. Once on the bus in may be difficult to find a seat and to know when to get off.

Sometimes when help is needed nobody can be found. Visually impaired people cannot always identify officials by their uniforms or badges. Taxis are a convenient form of transport but they are too expensive for many people to use very often and are difficult or impossible for visually impaired people to hail. In parts of Britain and other parts of the world, there are special buses for disabled people, like Dial-a-Ride in Britain, and subsidised taxi fares.

Sometimes people do not understand the problems visually impaired people face and may refuse to help or may give inappropriate assistance. Peter, talking about getting around in his school, said, 'I find going over to the west wing difficult...all the people are saying "watch it son" and "you're going to fall over" and I know that's not going to happen', and Chris said, 'They don't have announcements on buses and some of the bus drivers are dead arrogant. They said "you get off where you're supposed to get off, I haven't got time for all this."'

Visually impaired people, as you have seen, spend a great deal of their time and energy learning how to be mobile and coping with a hazardous environment when a lot of the problems could be resolved if their needs were taken into account. Crossing roads is far easier if there is a zebra crossing, an underpass, or traffic lights which bleep, and train and bus travel becomes more relaxing if the driver or guard announces the stops. Timetables can be taped, enlarged or transcribed into braille, and there are even some bus stops that 'talk'.

In some parts of the world visually impaired people are being assisted by the use of textured surfaces under foot so they can identify where traffic lights are located. Greater care is being taken to provide good lighting and distinct colours on trains and buses to assist visually impaired people. Many staff who work on the transport system now undergo *Disability Awareness Training* where they learn to understand the difficulties disabled people experience and how to assist them. Many of these strategies could be further enhanced, for example by providing tactile cues in shopping centres. Perhaps the most important way in which everyone can help is to keep the pavements clear of unnecessary obstacles. Problems of mobility do not lie within visually impaired people themselves but within the environment where their needs and rights are not taken into account.

Many of these changes would help a lot of other people too. Knowing where buses are going and what point in the journey they have reached would benefit, not only visually impaired people, but also visitors and those new to the area. Pedestrian crossings make the environment safer for everyone, and uncluttered pavements would help people using wheelchairs or those pushing pushchairs and prams. It would also make the environment more pleasant for us all. Care should be taken, however, when attempting to make areas more attractive; as you have seen plant pots, raised gardens, statues, benches, and wide open spaces themselves can create mobility barriers for visually impaired people.

Activity 6: Getting around

Have you ever had to wait ages for a bus or perhaps even got on the wrong one? We can all experience difficulties getting out and about to do the shopping and so on. Too much traffic can make it difficult crossing roads, and queues can make life difficult for us all. Though visually impaired people can get out and about more easily than sighted people might expect, many experience difficulties, particularly if they are unfamiliar with the journey, and many feel unable to leave their homes alone. The difficulties in getting out and about are important because they can have all kinds of consequences. Favourable changes to transport and the environment could transform visually impaired people's lives, and also make life easier for sighted people. In this Activity, then, let's think about the barriers that visually impaired people face in getting about the busy streets and some possible solutions in overcoming the barriers they encounter.

Q What might happen if there was no public transport?

Things to do

Imagine that there was no public transport. It might be that all the public transport workers have gone on strike. To make things worse, there is also a world shortage of petrol. Write down some of the main consequences that this situation would have for people's lives.

Hints

There would, of course, be many consequences for people. Not being able to get about is a barrier to many things. Some people would not be able to get into work, or school, or get the shopping as easily.

Q What does getting out and about involve?

Things to do

List the stages you go through when visiting a particular friend. Think of every aspect of your journey from leaving your home to meeting your friend. If possible include the use of public transport in your journey.

Hints

Your list will depend on where you live and the public transport you use. Sometimes we notice what such a journey involves when something goes wrong, such as a change in the weather, or particularly busy traffic.

Q What are the barriers that visually impaired people can face in getting out and about the streets?

Things to do

Look again at the journey you described. Make a list of the barriers you think visually impaired people might encounter if they attempted the same journey.

Hints

The following are some of the types of barriers you might have noted:

❑ pavements that are full of obstacles such as parked cars, holes and uneven surfaces and children's bicycles

❑ crossing roads

❑ recognising that a vehicle is a bus rather than say a large lorry

❑ knowing the bus number

❑ coping with large queues and crowded buses

❑ knowing where to get off.

You may have noted that the difficulties of a journey depend, in part, on how familiar we are with the route or area and how easy it would be to get information. You may have also noted that the barriers visually impaired people can encounter can also cause difficulties for sighted people. Have you ever seen a family with young children and a pushchair struggle to get on or off a bus? The obstacles can be particularly difficult for visually impaired people, however. Some obstacles are dangerous, especially for totally blind people and people who became visually impaired later in life.

Accidents caused by holes in the pavement or children's bikes blocking the path can result in injuries such as broken legs. Some visually impaired people are afraid to leave the relative safety of their own homes in case they have an accident and are injured.

Q What changes might be made to remove the barriers that visually impaired people face in getting out and about?

Things to do

Return to your list of barriers. Now list three ways in which the barriers you identified could be removed.

Hints

There are many possibilities and you may have noticed that an environment which would be better for visually impaired people would generally be a better environment for everyone. No-one, for instance, likes overcrowded buses. Your list might have included the following:

❑ a campaign to clear the pavements of obstacles

❑ more bleeper crossings and underpasses

❑ announcements to say when a bus is coming and where it is going

❑ more staff to help people on buses

❑ announcements telling people where the bus is each time it stops.

Seventeen: Education

People have many different experiences of schools: some happy and some not so happy. There are important things for us all about going to school: friendships and relationships with other pupils; teachers we like or don't like; subjects we are good at or not; and so on. The same things are, of course, important for visually impaired young people. The difference is that many visually impaired young people experience segregated schooling.

A separate system of special schools and colleges has developed in many countries, for example schools and colleges that cater only for visually impaired people. Some visually impaired children go to other kinds of special school, such as schools for children who have learning difficulties. This is because many visually impaired children have other impairments such as a hearing impairment or a learning difficulty. This separate system of education means that visually impaired people either have to travel a long way each day to attend a special school or have to live at a boarding school. This began in Europe in the late eighteenth and early nineteenth century. The schools were often run by charities or religious groups. Many segregated schools were opened in European countries following the Second World War, particularly boarding schools. The idea grew that visually impaired children needed special help in special schools. In more recent years, segregated systems have emerged in other countries, with for instance the South African National Council for the Blind providing 16 separate schools for the 'upbringing, education and training of visually disabled children.' Ved Mehta has written a very interesting book about the four years he spent at a boarding school for visually impaired children in Bombay between 1938 and 1942. From the age of four he lived 900 miles from his family in the school which was also an orphanage. In some countries many visually impaired children do not go to school at all. In Tanzania only 10 per cent of visually impaired children go to school. You may remember that Ayesha did not go to school when she lived in India, although there were a few special boarding schools for visually impaired pupils.

In recent years in many European countries, increasing numbers of young visually impaired people have attended ordinary or what are often called 'mainstream' schools. Mainstream schools sometimes have special units within them for visually impaired pupils. You may remember that Chris and Peter attended such a unit in their school.

So what do visually impaired people say about their experiences of school, particularly about the difficulties they face? Amer Mukaram, who is head of the Youth Association of the Blind in Lebanon and was blinded in a shooting accident at the age of seven, says: 'I come from a mountain village, and from the time I became blind I was cut off completely from my home environment. My relatives considered that I was ill. The school for the blind that I attended was a welfare school. There was no contact with family or friends at home...It took me years after I left to learn how to relate to people normally.' (Coleridge 1993).

The education of visually impaired young people

In 1992 in Britain: 53 per cent of visually impaired young people went to mainstream schools; 22 per cent went to a special or residential school for visually impaired pupils; 24 per cent went to other kinds of schools. The Royal National Institute for the Blind runs five special schools and is the largest provider of special schools for visually impaired children in Britain.

In Spain in 1992: 83 per cent of visually impaired young people went to mainstream schools; and 17 per cent went to special day or residential schools for visually impaired pupils.

This is a common experience for many visually impaired young people who attend special schools, particularly boarding schools. Many special schools are boarding schools because of the relatively low numbers of visually impaired children, particularly in the developed countries where visual impairment is among the rarest of impairments in young people. Until recent times children who boarded were not allowed to go home very much during term time, but now most go home at weekends.

So many visually impaired children do not go to the same schools as sighted young people who live in their neighbourhoods or the same schools as sighted brothers and sisters. Think about your own friends. It is quite likely that many of your friends go to the same school as you and live close enough for you to see them outside school in the evenings, weekends and holidays. Young people who go to special schools do not have the same opportunities to meet and make friends with sighted young people who live close by.

It can also be difficult to see school friends because they live too far away. Sometimes this is also true for young people who, like Peter, go to mainstream schools, particularly when they have to travel to a school with a special unit. Nevertheless it is young people who attend boarding schools who experience the most extreme form of separation. Like Amer Mukaram they can feel separated from their whole family as well as from other young people in the community.

Young visually impaired people can experience many barriers in schools. In mainstream schools, particularly, they can face the sorts of negative attitudes we discussed earlier from both other pupils and teachers. This can include teasing and bullying, being excluded from activities (such as physical education), being made to join in activities which are very difficult for visually impaired people, or being made to feel inferior. They face learning barriers in lessons in which, for instance, there is a lot of working from the blackboard or use of detailed diagrams that are not made accessible to them. Visually impaired pupils can also find it very difficult working with sighted pupils when they cannot do the work as quickly as them. Stephanie spoke of these problems at her school.

Many visually impaired young people, particularly those who attend special schools, do not feel that their education prepares them very well for adult life. Mary, a visually impaired person we spoke to, told us, 'I didn't have enough experience of life...I was terrified because I didn't know how to handle adult relationships.' There is also a lack of educational opportunities when leaving school. The choice for a sighted young person can be difficult enough, but visually impaired young people have far less choice. Many colleges do not cater for visually impaired students and special colleges are few and far between. In some countries, such as China, visually impaired people are not accepted at university.

There are many arguments for and many against having special schools. Two arguments for special schools and colleges are:

❑ Special schools and colleges provide a special environment which is adapted to the needs of visually impaired young people, with special equipment, special resources and help from teachers and other professionals who know about their special needs.

❑ Special schools and colleges are places where visually impaired young people can be with others who face the same problems as themselves.

Two arguments against segregation are:

❑ It is a system which separates young visually impaired people from young sighted people. It makes young visually impaired people feel different and separate and it makes sighted young people feel that visually impaired young people are different from themselves.

❑ Father Cutinha is the director of the Divine Light Trust which was set up as a school for visually impaired children in Southern India. He explains why he is against special schools in India: 'Take our institution here. It started as a school. But after 35 years of running it as a school, it came as a severe trauma to me to discover that only about 5 per cent of blind children are in blind schools...We were not even beginning to touch the problem.' (Coleridge 1993).

So this whole question of whether there should be special schools, or whether resources should be put into making mainstream schools accessible to visually impaired people, is very controversial. Some people believe that both special and mainstream schools and colleges should be available to visually impaired people to give them maximum choice.

The creation of a barrier-free learning environment is another question to which people have given a lot of thought. What would a school be like if it catered for visually impaired as well as sighted young people?

❑ Every teacher in the school, with training and support, would be prepared and able to teach visually impaired as well as sighted young people.

❑ There would be help and support for visually impaired pupils when they needed it. Pupils would not, however, be made to feel different or inferior because of their different working methods or their need for extra adult attention.

Special further education colleges

There are three special further education colleges for visually impaired students in Britain: RNIB's Redhill College in Surrey; Queen Alexandra College in Birmingham; and The Royal National College for the Blind in Hereford. So most young people who wish to go to a special college have to move a considerable distance from their homes.

❑ The school buildings and all the activities within the school would be fully accessible to all pupils. The use of raised diagrams, for example, would make areas of maths such as geometry available to visually impaired young people.

❑ The attitudes of the sighted pupils would be positive towards visually impaired people. Disability awareness programmes may be helpful, though they have to be done very carefully as attitudes are very difficult to change.

❑ Finally it may be important for visually impaired young people to share their experiences with other visually impaired young people. They can, for instance, talk about the barriers they face and the changes that are needed to create a barrier-free learning environment.

Quote Senda 2003

Activity 7: A question of schools

Schooling is important to us all. We spend a lot of time when we are young actually in school, and school has an influence on our lives and experiences as adults. There are many different types of schools, including, for instance, schools for girls, schools for boys, schools for Catholic children, private schools which parents pay for their children to attend, and special schools which are intended for disabled young people. Furthermore, young people's experiences in schools differ considerably. Some look back on it as the best time of their lives, but other people remember their schools lives with little happiness. This Activity is about the different experiences young people have, the different type of schools and the changes that may be needed in mainstream schools so that visually impaired and sighted young people can be educated together. You may already have visually impaired pupils in your school. This might make this Activity a little easier, but in any case you should be able to tackle the questions and do the exercises.

Q Could visually impaired pupils attend your school and be educated together with sighted pupils?

Things to do

Do a review of what your school might or might not provide for visually impaired pupils. First, write down five strengths of your school, that is all the things about your school which would make it a good school for visually impaired pupils. Second, write down five weaknesses, that is things about your school which would make things difficult for visually impaired pupils.

Hints

As usual you may have noticed that these strengths and weaknesses can be similar for sighted people. For instance, if one of the strengths of your school is that the pupils are friendly then this would be good for sighted as well as visually impaired pupils. If, on the other hand, one of the weaknesses is bullies, then of course this is bad for sighted pupils as well. The kinds of things you might have mentioned in both lists include:

❏ the relationships between pupils, and between pupils and teachers

❏ whether or not lessons are interesting and well taught

❏ whether pupils receive help if they experience difficulties

❏ the attitudes of pupils and teachers.

Q What are the advantages and disadvantages of special and mainstream schools?

Things to do

Make a list of what you and other pupils get from attending your school. Try to identify five of the main things.

Next make a list of the things you think that visually impaired young people might get from attending a special school.

Then compare the two lists.

Hints

Some of the items in these lists could be similar. Schools, for instance, are important for everyone for making and being with friends. Being helped to learn is also important for everyone. The differences in the two lists might have included such things as specialist help for visually impaired pupils in special schools. One way of thinking about the integration of visually impaired pupils in mainstream schools is that mainstream schools should provide the sort of support and resources that are found in special schools.

Q What changes need to be made in mainstream schools so that visually impaired young people can be educated together with sighted pupils?

Things to do

Write down five ways in which your school might be improved, by removing the barriers, so it would be better for visually impaired pupils.

Hints

You may have noted that visually impaired young people themselves could be asked about the support they need. It is also important to note that no two visually impaired young people will need exactly the same support. Your list might have included such things as:

❑ alternatives to work on the blackboard, such as having information on the blackboard put into print, on to tape or in braille, or simply having someone read it aloud

❑ the provision of support in the classroom either from teachers or other pupils

❑ the removal of obstacles from corridors and so on

❑ the provision of a room where visually impaired pupils might meet.

It is important to remember that visually impaired pupils will be able to return the support in different ways, for example by offering help to others with a subject they are particularly good at. Visually impaired pupils, like sighted pupils, can contribute to the school as a whole.

A visually impaired student in higher education

Eighteen: Different individuals – Geoff

 Geoff is 75 and lives in the south of England. He was born with a hereditary eye condition which his father, brother, sister and aunt also had. When Geoff was born he had full sight, but by the time he was 13 years old he was totally blind in one eye and partially sighted in the other. Geoff went to a mainstream school where he could see what was going on from the front of the classroom. He enjoyed cricket and football and played for the school teams. Geoff is totally blind now but his gradual loss of sight never worried him because he expected it. He said: 'I took it in my stride. I've never bothered about it at all. You hear people on the television and radio saying how difficult it would be and how awful it would be, but it never bothered me.'

Geoff left school when he was 14 and worked in a grocery shop in London. He managed very well, cutting up the food and serving the customers, but as his sight deteriorated he began to find it more difficult. He could not recognise the customers or read the shopping lists they gave him.

When Geoff was 33 he decided the time had come to train for another job. There was not much choice of occupation for visually impaired people and he was advised to train as a braille shorthand typist. Geoff studied in a small class with six other visually impaired people, and at the end of the training he found a job in the Civil Service. He was paid more than he had been in the shop but did not like the work nearly as much.

Geoff worked as a braille shorthand typist for thirteen years. He was then given the opportunity to train as a computer programmer which was a new field of work for visually impaired people at that time. Geoff worked as a computer programmer until he retired. He enjoyed the work a lot more than the shorthand typing.

When Geoff was young his favourite pastimes were greyhound racing, cinema and playing cards. He also enjoyed drama and took the lead part in four plays produced by a drama group of visually impaired people. He now enjoys talking books (book on audiotape), listening to music and sport on the radio, and going on holiday. Geoff is married and has a son and a granddaughter. He is helped to get around by his guide dog, Leon.

Nineteen: Employment

Visually impaired people are employed in all sorts of occupations. The visually impaired adults we spoke to were all working or had worked. You may remember that Martha worked as a school teacher and a braille proof reader. The other visually impaired people had quite a wide variety of jobs; Louise went to university and became a psychiatric social worker, Mike worked in a shop but later became a sound technician; and Paul is the manager of a small charity. Sue, Mary and Alan have all been involved in clerical work, and Ayesha is a college lecturer. Alan and Mike have also experienced self-employment.

Visually impaired people have taken their place in many professions throughout the world as physiotherapists, lawyers, politicians and musicians. In most countries of the world, visually impaired people are, however, much more likely to be unemployed than sighted people. There are a few jobs which visually impaired people cannot do, for example bus driving and surgery, but for the most part people are excluded, not because they are incapable of doing the work, but because of the many barriers which stand in their way. These include lack of access to information, lack of suitable equipment, negative attitudes from employers, lack of transport to get to work, and the ways in which tasks are carried out. Employers often focus on the inabilities of visually impaired people rather than their abilities, and sometimes confuse visual impairment with illness. Visually impaired people do not, of course, feel ill through lack of sight and may be very fit and healthy. It is interesting that at times of war, when many non-disabled people are fighting, disabled people have successfully carried out many responsible jobs which, when the war is over, they nearly always lose.

Even if visually impaired people find work, their choice is often very limited; they are frequently told *what* to do rather than being asked what they would *like* to do. Louise said, 'It tended to be either physiotherapy, secretarial work, or going to university. I went to university because it was assumed I would. I don't remember any discussion about it.' The *All India Confederation of the Blind* told us that most visually impaired

Work rates

Spain has the highest employment rate for visually impaired people in the world, approximately 75 per cent of those of working age. A large proportion work for the *Spanish National Association for the Blind*. In Britain approximately 25% of visually impaired people of working age are employed. The highest proportion work as telephonists but others work as physiotherapists, lawyers, lecturers, clerical workers and factory workers. In Korea approximately 7 per cent of visually impaired people of working age are in employment. Most people work as masseurs, acupuncturists and fortune tellers.

people are restricted to work in traditional crafts because of lack of facilities to train for other occupations.

The work that visually impaired people do is often, though not always, poorly paid. Many people work in sheltered workshops, where they do not need to be as productive as they would in open (ordinary) employment, and where their wages may be little more than pocket money. This is a serious state of affairs because visually impaired people need more, rather than less money, so that they can buy services to help them with tasks such as reading print, house maintenance and travel. In some countries, for example Australia, visually impaired people are given an allowance from the government to help with these extra costs and in Britain many visually impaired people are eligible for the Disability Living Allowance, but for many people there is no assistance from the government at all.

As well as earning money, there are other advantages to being employed. Having a job gives a structure to the day, provides company and friendship and gives people dignity, status and a feeling of being useful. It prevents boredom and isolation and can give people the opportunity to develop their talents. This is not to say that voluntary work and leisure activities are less important, but in most countries today work is given great emphasis, particularly in places where the government provides little or no help in times of difficulty. Martha says of Malaysia: 'There is no welfare system there so everyone has to fend for themselves.' Lack of employment can lead to poverty, isolation, ill health and feelings of uselessness. Aslad Daud from Palestine believes that work is essential, he says: 'You cannot give people their rights by giving them money...Money does not defend him. What defends him is his job, his work. If he has a job, he is living proof that he is a human being like everyone else.' (Coleridge 1993)

All the visually impaired adults we spoke to commented on the barriers they had faced in employment. Martha left her teaching job because she had no equipment or help with all the reading she was expected to do, and Alan left his clerical job because he

Among the many professions open to visually impaired people are teaching and DJ-ing

was expected to work at a faster pace than he was able to achieve. He also found meetings very difficult because he could not see people's body language.

Most of these barriers can be removed with imagination, a positive attitude and sufficient resources. If Martha had equipment to enlarge print, or had received help to pay people to read to her, she would have found her teaching job less stressful. If Alan was permitted to take more time over his work, or was given some assistance, he might not have left. Sometimes it is work colleagues who can make all the difference to a visually impaired person. Mike told us that he asks his colleagues to help him on occasions and that he can, of course, help them in other ways.

Many of the visually impaired people we spoke to had specialised equipment and financial help from government to assist them at work. This included computer equipment which enlarged print, 'talked', and produced braille. Some people had scanners which read print aloud, machines which enlarge print, and money to pay for people to read to them. Many of these services are provided in Britain by the government's 'Access to Work' scheme.

In many parts of the world resources and services such as these are not available or are in short supply. In Ethiopia, for example, work for visually impaired people is so scarce that they are often forced into begging for a living, and in Lebanon the government will not employ anyone who is ill or disabled, except for a few visually impaired telephonists who have no rights or hope of promotion (Coleridge 1993). Yet people do not sit back helplessly when assistance is not available. *The Tanzania Society for the Blind* runs a farm where visually impaired people are trained and employed, and in many parts of the world, for example Poland and Spain, schools and associations for visually impaired people teach them a trade or profession, such as piano tuning, physiotherapy, computer programming, knitting, and telephony.

Twenty: Changing the world

A priority in many developing countries is the prevention of impairments of the eye. The numbers of visually impaired people are large and many have conditions which could be cured if medical and social resources were available. The Tanzania Society for the Blind, for instance, co-ordinates all the visual impairment prevention programmes. It gives support to mobile eye care clinics, and river blindness and trachoma (see Glossary p71-4) control programmes. About 50 per cent of blindness in Tanzania is caused by cataracts. Modern surgical techniques mean that cataract operations are both simple and quick, taking less than half an hour. After-care is needed but people's sight can be fully restored.

Disabled people want the removal of the environmental and social barriers which prevent them from participating in the community's daily life: they want control over their own lives rather than being forced into dependency. One change towards achieving this would be the introduction of anti-discrimination legislation. This legislation has already been introduced in many countries, including: Australia, the USA, Canada and New Zealand. It has recently been introduced, in a limited form, in Britain. The legislation is a way of trying to make people provide equal opportunities for disabled people. Similar legislation exists in some countries to provide equal opportunities for men and women, and for people from ethnic minorities, for example the Sex Discrimination Act 1986 and the Race Relations Act 1976 in Britain. Paul told us: 'There's got to be legislation which makes it obligatory for people to provide information in a medium (large print, braille and so on) that you want. At least the stuff that you ask for or the stuff that you are getting from the bank, or the building society, or the council, or the tax man, or whatever would come in a medium that you could read.'

Can attitudes be changed and if so how? Attitudes of any kind are difficult to change. One approach is called 'simulation'. To simulate blindness, for instance, would involve walking around for a while with a blindfold on. However, this has not proved to be a successful way of changing attitudes. Disability Equality Training works in a different way. This involves disabled trainers talking about a social model of disability and disabled people's own experiences. For widespread change to occur, it would be necessary for disability equality training to be available to all young people and adults who have contact with visually impaired people.

Twenty-one: Different Individuals – Ayesha

Ayesha was born in a rural village in India in 1965. She has been blind since she was four years old as a result of meningitis. There were no other visually impaired people living in the village and Ayesha was not allowed to go to school with the other children. Instead she spent a lot of time with her neighbours, looking after their babies and young children and helping with the cooking and washing. The neighbours gave Ayesha a lot of kindness and encouragement, but she longed to go to school. Many people in the village thought it was impossible for visually impaired people to learn everyday skills and to be independent, but Ayesha never believed them.

Ayesha had no white cane or guide dog to help her get around the village, but she did not find it difficult. There were no roads or traffic and no lamp posts in the way. The only danger came from snakes and scorpions. Some of the snakes in the village, such as giant cobras, could kill with their venom.

Ayesha came to England with her family when she was 14 and went to school for the first time. It was a boarding school for visually impaired pupils. Before she could go to school Ayesha had home tuition in English and braille; she had never used braille before, but learned to read and write it very quickly. Ayesha found it difficult at school at first because the other children made fun of her Asian clothes, her different diet and the way she spoke English, but she soon made friends. Ayesha was so pleased to be at school that she worked very hard to pass her examinations and did very well.

When she left school Ayesha went to a residential college for visually impaired students to take some more examinations. From there she went to university where she studied social policy and race relations. She had to work very hard because working in braille is slower than working in print and the lecturers were not always helpful about reading what they had written on the blackboard or giving her booklists in advance.

After leaving university Ayesha worked for three years in the field of race relations and then as a lecturer in her local college teaching English as a second language, and race and disability issues. Ayesha is now completing some research into the experiences of disabled women from ethnic minorities. When it is finished she hopes to become a university lecturer and writer. Ayesha lives in central England with her husband. She is helped to get around by her guide dog Lindy.

Twenty-two: Getting together for a change

Whenever there is widespread dissatisfaction among a section of society they tend to come together as a group to press for change. If the group becomes large and politically active it is known as a social movement. A social movement may consist of many small groups of people all working towards a common goal.

It has been very difficult for disabled people to come together and have an influence on how society is run. This is because they have been segregated in different institutions according to their impairments. They also lack public and private transport, and have always been among the poorest members of society. As facilities have gradually improved in many countries over the last 20 years, disabled people have come together to campaign for change and a strong Disabled People's Movement has emerged. The Disabled People's Movement aims to dismantle disabling barriers and to empower disabled people by enabling them to see that disability is created by barriers within society, rather than by something which is wrong with them.

The Disabled People's Movement consists of many small organisations with similar aims throughout the world. These organisations are run and controlled by disabled people themselves although many welcome non-disabled allies. Amer Mukaram of the *Youth Association of the Blind* in Palestine says:

'We reject the idea of forming an association only for visually impaired people. We must enlist sighted volunteers in our organisation and develop friendships between blind and sighted people so that they understand each other.' (Coleridge 1993).

In 1981 *Disabled People's International* was founded. This is an umbrella organisation which represents and unites disabled people throughout the world. Rachel Hurst, who is the president of the organisation, says:

'When you come together with other disabled people, you have the time and the opportunity to discuss what the situation really is – what oppression is, who is oppressing you, where oppression comes from, what discrimination is and where it comes from.' (Coleridge 1993).

Disabled people only feel oppressed when they are *forced* to live, work or study together by non-disabled people. When they come together by choice it can be a liberating experience. Khalfan Khalfan, for example, was inspired to found the *Association of Disabled People of Zanzibar* after meeting disabled people from all over the world at a conference in Singapore. On occasions, active associations have stemmed from the dissatisfaction of disabled people living in segregated institutions. This is how the Disabled People's Movement in Zimbabwe started. It is now one of the strongest Disabled People's Movement in Africa. In Lebanon the Disabled People's Movement was triggered by the large numbers of people disabled in the war. It also attracted many other disabled people and has become the strongest Disabled People's Movement in the Middle East (Coleridge 1993). Even in the most difficult circumstances creativity and social change can occur.

Visually impaired people have taken their place within the Disabled People's Movement alongside deaf people, those with motor impairments, people with learning difficulties and many others. Some of the organisations within the movement are working specifically to improve the lives of visually impaired people. Both India and Britain, for example, have an organisation called the *National Federation of the Blind* which is run and controlled by visually impaired people.

It is recognised, however, that there are many issues which need to be fought collectively such as prejudice and discrimination, lack of appropriate education, lack of employment opportunities, lack of rehabilitation for those people who become visually impaired, and an inaccessible environment. Although the Disability People's Movement has flourished in recent years, the fight by disabled people to improve their lives is by no means new. One of the early groups in Britain, which was founded in 1898, was the *National League of the Blind*. This was a very militant trade union which campaigned hard to improve working conditions for visually impaired people at that time. The organisation still exists today as *The National League of the Blind and Disabled*.

The Disabled People's Movement has been active in many ways. It has pressed for legislation to be passed to outlaw discrimination against disabled people which in some parts of the world, for example Sweden and the USA, has been successful. It has organised conferences to discuss disability issues, such as poor job opportunities, and has undertaken research to demonstrate the widespread discrimination which disabled people face within society. It has set up services run and controlled by disabled people, for example, to give advice, information and counselling. Sometimes direct action has been taken where disabled people have protested by chanting and displaying banners, or chaining themselves to buses to draw attention to the inaccessibility of public transport. As we have seen, in some countries, for example Tanzania and Ethiopia, visual impairment is very widespread and is caused by diseases, such as cataracts, glaucoma and river blindness, which could be cured or reduced if the necessary will and resources were available. A great deal of effort is therefore spent by organisations of visually impaired people in these countries, in trying to prevent unnecessary visual impairment.

All of these activities help disabled people to feel strong, capable and good about themselves which, in turn, strengthens the Disabled People's Movement because people are no longer afraid to fight for what they need. Disabled people have sometimes felt negative about themselves because that is how other people have viewed and treated them. Involvement in the Disabled People's Movement has helped many disabled people to overcome these feelings. This is expressed by B Venkatesh (Venky) the Director of *Action on Disability and Development in India*. He says:

'The primary aim of my work is to enable disabled people to feel good about themselves. How people feel about themselves has a direct impact on what they do and how they do it. Unless they feel good about themselves they won't be able to do very much.' (Coleridge 1993).

Alan thinks that anti-discrimination legislation is the most important way forward for visually impaired people, and Louise says, 'There needs to be disability rights legislation particularly over employment.' The same views are expressed by Amer Mukaram who says, 'The law must make it possible for disabled people to enjoy the rights that other people have.' It is a sad truth that no government has ever given rights to disabled people willingly. Change only comes about when disabled people get together and exert pressure as a group.

Twenty-three: Different individuals – Mike

Mike was born visually impaired. Initially he went to a mainstream school but could not see to read the blackboard or work as fast as the other pupils; the class was very large and Mike was given very little help.

When he was nine Mike went to a boarding school for visually impaired children in the west of England. He felt happy there because his needs were understood, but the education was very basic. Mike could only go home for one weekend in four and as a result he became rather detached from his family and community; his brother played with lots of boys who Mike knew nothing about. He did not feel isolated though because he had lots of hobbies. He loved reading and while he was at the special school he produced the school magazine and started a photography club.

Mike left school when he was 16 and worked in an office for a short time and then in a shop. His real interest, however, was engineering. After five or six years in the shop Mike answered a job advertisement for an audio-technician at his local university; he was offered the job and remains there today. Mike has a particular interest in sound recording. He makes recordings, teaches students and staff to make their own recordings and builds and maintains equipment. He also has his own successful part-time sound recording business which he runs from home. It sometimes gets so busy that it is hard to fit everything in! Mike is so interested in his work that it has become his hobby too, and leaves him with little time to spare.

The biggest problem Mike finds about being visually impaired is that life is geared to people who own cars and can drive. Sometimes he cannot go out in the evening because there is no way of getting home late at night, and he finds it difficult to attend concerts and other functions at his daughter's school. The big, local shopping stores are also awkward to get to without a car. What Mike would like to see most of all is a good public transport system so that he would have as much freedom as people who can drive.

Twenty-four: What visually impaired people are doing

As you read earlier, disabled people are increasingly joining together to campaign for change. They are also coming together to help each other express themselves in music, drama, forms of visual art and comedy. Through disability arts many visually impaired people have regular opportunities to share ideas and information with each other and other disabled people. As we saw earlier, many of the images in the media, and disabled characters in books and films have promoted negative stereotypes.

Gary Sargeant, a visually impaired fine artist, has exhibited his work both in Britain and abroad

Through their writing and visual and performing arts, disabled people are promoting very different images which celebrate differences between people and the value of all people.

Gohar Kordi was born in Iran. She became totally blind at the age of three. Though she could not attend a school until she was 14, she was the first blind woman to enter the University of Tehran. Her autobiography and the two novels she wrote have been

After Blenheim by Jennifer Maskell Packer

published and she has written a stage play. Her story, 'I Was Touched', which is about her experiences, was included in *Mustn't Grumble* which is a book of writings (poems, stories and so on) by disabled women. It ends as follows: 'Touch can be so beautiful to me. Sometimes my son is cruel. But at other times he flings his arms around me and kisses me on the eyes and says, "Mummy, I love you, you are the best mummy in the world." His touch, the tenderness, lift me right above the clouds, into the sunlight. They warm me right through and I just float, and I forget all the troubles of the world, and all the suffering is worth it for these moments.' (Keith 1994)

Art ventures

There is a specific drama group of visually impaired people in London called 'The Venturers' which regularly puts on plays. There are also two Disability Arts magazines in Britain, 'Disability Arts in London' and 'Disability Arts Magazine'.

Barbara Kendrick has also been visually impaired since early childhood. She lives with her husband and two children in Ohio in America. She has written articles and poetry and is the editor of *Tactic*, a computer journal for visually impaired people. Her short story, '20/20 with a twist', was included in another anthology of writing by disabled women called *With Wings*. It is a story which is set in the future, in a world which has changed a lot for visually impaired people.

'From the dark-age days of the nineties, the blind had finally achieved their long-deserved status in education and employment and had secured a Department of Visual Equality in the bargain.' (Saxton and Howe 1988).

The idea of Disability Arts is about disabled people communicating their thoughts, feelings and experiences. As it grows worldwide, it will challenge prejudice, discrimination and oppression.

Activity 8: What have you learned and what next?

There are many ideas for you to think about in this book. We hope you feel you have a better understanding of the lives and experiences of visually impaired people. But we also hope that you do <u>not</u> feel you know all there is to know about visual impairment, and that you want to keep thinking, finding out more and supporting visually impaired people. This Activity is a little different from other Activities in this book. It is about returning to and reviewing some of the main ideas you have been thinking about. There are no *Things to do*, except you should flick back through the book as you think about the questions. In particular, re-read about the different individuals: Chris, Stephanie, Martha, Sally, Geoff, Ayesha and Mike. The *Hints* are our answers to the questions we have set to help you review your thinking and ideas.

Q How can you find out about the lives and experiences of visually impaired people?

Hints
Sighted people do not have direct experience of being visually impaired. Sighted people cannot know what it means to be visually impaired by closing their eyes or wearing a blindfold. You can always open your eyes again or take off the blindfold. This is not what it is like to be visually impaired. The best way to find out is to listen to visually impaired people, or read what they have to say.

Q In what ways are the lives and experiences of visually impaired and sighted people similar, and in what ways are they different?

Hints
The first thing to say is that visually impaired and sighted people are first and foremost people. There is much that is and can be shared: the pleasures of friendship; hopes for the future; co-operating and competing with others; enjoyment and the frustrations of work and leisure; enjoyment and frustrations of learning, teaching, helping and receiving help; and so on. As people, being sighted or visually impaired makes no difference.

But there are differences in the lives of sighted and visually impaired people. You have been reading about many of them and about the 'social model of disability' which explains these differences. Visually impaired people face barriers, restrictions, prejudices and a lack of opportunities which can prevent them from leading full lives. Not to be able to walk down the street because there are holes in the pavement or because dustbins have been left in the way makes life different for visually impaired people. Not to be able to go to mainstream school because of a lack of resources and support makes life different for visually impaired people. Not to be able to get a job because an employer thinks visually impaired people cannot or should not work makes life different for visually impaired people. We hope you can add to this list.

Q In what ways do visually impaired people differ from each other in their lives and experiences?

Hints
Throughout this book we have tried to show that the lives and experiences of visually impaired people depend on the society they live in. What it means to be visually impaired depends on where you live. It also depends on when you live, because as society changes so do the lives and experiences of visually impaired people. It depends, too, on the individual. Visually impaired people are all different people, just as sighted people are all individuals.

Q 'What can I do?'

Hints

There is a growing awareness, for some people at least, that we all bear a responsibility for the world we live in. Schools, for instance, in which some young people are bullied are bad schools, not just for those who are actually bullied, but for everyone involved with the school. Similarly, visual impairment is not just a concern for visually impaired people, it is a concern for us all. A world in which all visually impaired people can lead lives as full as sighted people would be a better world for us all. There are things we can all do and listening to visually impaired people is the first step. As a final *Things to do*, glance again at all the stories of the different individuals and make a list of the implications of what they say for you personally: the things that you could do. We shall look at this in the final section of the book.

Twenty-five: What can you do?

So what can you do? We are all involved with visual impairment. It is not a matter of eyes and how they work. It is about people. It is about creating a world in which visually impaired people are equal. It is about creating a world which is free of barriers and designed for everyone, so that people have the same opportunities in education and in work, leisure and in getting out and about; a world in which people do not have to face prejudice and negative attitudes just because they happen to be visually impaired. This is the ideal for which many visually impaired people are campaigning. Sighted people can make it their fight too and support visually impaired people in their struggle for a better world for everyone.

What do visually impaired people say about what you can do?

❑ 'Just treat me like a normal human being,' says Helen. She wants to be thought of and treated as a person in her own right not with a preconceived idea, or prejudice, about what it means to be visually impaired. 'If you know someone with a sight problem, you shouldn't think they are silly and stupid,' says Stephanie, 'it really is hard, sometimes, to do things.'

❑ 'Sight impaired people cope in different ways and it is necessary to treat people individually,' says Alan. Part of prejudice is the belief that all visually impaired people are the same because they are visually impaired. The truth is, as Alan says, all visually impaired people are different.

❏ Mike told us that sighted people should ask visually impaired people what help they want. 'Don't make assumptions,' he says. So the message is to listen to visually impaired people.

❏ Sighted people should 'make themselves known,' says Chris, 'either by a touch on the arm or using your name,' adds Sue. So make yourself known and listen: don't make assumptions about what it is like to be visually impaired or what help people might need, but do not be afraid to ask.

❏ If a visually impaired person would like you to help by guiding him or her across the road or to a shop, do not be afraid to ask how the person would like to be guided. Most visually impaired people will prefer to hold your arm just above your elbow. You should always lead the person from in front, never push him or her ahead of you. Explain things the visually impaired person cannot see, such as whether steps you are approaching go up or down.

❏ If you feel that you do not quite know what to do to help a visually impaired person, do not worry. The most important thing is that you are willing to help. Do not worry about getting it wrong, *just ask*.

❏ You can help visually impaired people by keeping streets safer and easier for everyone. For instance, do not leave bikes in the way and make sure that any trees or bushes that overhang a pavement are trimmed back.

❏ Finally, Peter says that sighted people do not know what it is like to be visually impaired: 'they do not know how to experience it and they are frightened.' Sighted people can learn something of what it is like to be visually impaired from the experiences of visually impaired people themselves.

You will not know what it is like to be visually impaired just because you have read this book: but we hope that you have started to understand what it means to be visually impaired and will want to find out more.

Most visually impaired people like to be guided by holding your arm just above the elbow

Glossary

AIDS (Acquired Immune Deficiency Syndrome): A viral disease which causes the body to lose its ability to resist infection. The disease can sometimes involve visual impairment.

Anti-discrimination legislation: A set of laws created by government which attempt to prevent the unfair treatment of certain groups such as people from ethnic minorities and disabled people.

Attitude: The way people think, feel and behave towards people and events.

Barrier: Something which prevents people from doing what they want to do.

Blind: A person is blind if he or she has no eyesight.

Body language: Communication which does not involve the use of words. This includes facial expression, posture, and gestures like nodding and waving.

Braille: A system of writing for visually impaired people comprising six raised dots in different combinations which are read by touch. Braille enables many visually impaired people to read and write.

Cataract: A disease which causes clouding of the lens of the eye leading to visual impairment. It usually affects old people.

Charity: Money or goods given to people who are poor or disadvantaged. A charity is an organisation which raises money for this purpose, and provides goods and services to the people concerned.

Culture: The customs, ideas and art of a particular society or group of people.

D

Developing countries: Countries which are developing economically but which remain poor.

Diabetes: A disease where the body fails to produce sufficient insulin. This can result in visual impairment.

Disability arts: A cultural activity where disabled people express their views and experiences of disability through songs, drama, painting and comedy. These views often challenge what non-disabled people believe about disability.

Disability awareness/equality training: Training which people undertake to understand the problems disabled people face, the causes of these problems, and the help which can be offered.

Disabled People's Movement: A social movement of disabled people who, through political activity and disability arts, aim to change society by breaking down barriers which stand in the way of them leading full lives. The Disabled People's Movement links disabled people from all over the world.

Discriminate: To treat a particular person or group of people badly or unfairly.

E

Empower: To gain the authority and skills to make choices and to control one's own life.

G

Guide dog: A dog which is trained to guide visually impaired people.

Glaucoma: A disease in which there is increased pressure in the eye. It usually appears after the age of forty and can lead to visual impairment.

H

Hereditary eye condition: An eye condition which is passed down to children from their parents through the genes.

I

Identity: All the characteristics, attitudes, talents and personality, which make up a person. To have a positive identity means to feel good about oneself.

Ill: Being unhealthy. Feeling unwell.

Individual model of disability: A view of disability, put forward by non-disabled people, that the problems disabled people face result from their impairments and that to have these impairments is to be abnormal.

L

Long white cane: A white cane which is used by visually impaired people to find steps and kerbs and to ensure that the ground in front of them is clear of obstacles.

M

Macular degeneration: A disease where there is gradual destruction of the macular (a very important area of the retina of the eye). It usually affects old people and leads to visual impairment.

Mainstream schools: Schools which the majority of young people attend.

Mobile eye clinic: A clinic, used in developing countries, where people can have their eyes treated medically. Mobile clinics are situated in large vehicles which travel to remote areas where medical assistance is limited.

Moon: A system of writing for visually impaired people comprising raised shapes which are read by touch. Moon enables many visually impaired people to read and write.

Oppression: To treat people cruelly, unfairly or unjustly. To keep them down.

P

Partially sighted: A person is partially sighted if he or she has a small but useful amount of eye sight.

Physiotherapy: Medical treatment which involves manipulation, massage, exercise and electrical treatment.

Prejudice: To pre-judge a person or group of people without knowing very much about them. It usually refers to an unfair judgement.

R

Rehabilitation: A form of training where people are taught a variety of skills to help them lead full lives.

Rights: Moral or legal entitlements: People in most countries, for example, have a right to go to school.

River blindness (Onchocerciasis): River blindness is caused by a worm which lives in the human body and is transmitted by the black fly. People can become infected by the worm either by direct contact with it or by tainted water. The infection causes inflammation and scarring of the cornea (outer transparent part of the eye) leading to visual impairment.

S

Segregated schools: Schools where young disabled people with specific impairments, for example visual impairment, may attend.

Simulate: An attempt to imitate something. A person may try to simulate blindness by wearing a blindfold.

Stereotype: To stereotype a person is to assume that he or she is a particular type of person who will think and behave in specific ways.

Social model of disability: A view of disability, put forward by disabled people, that the problems disabled people face result from barriers within society.

Social movement: A group of people who come together in large numbers to bring about fundamental changes in society.

Symbol white cane: A short white cane which is used to let other people know that the person is visually impaired.

Trachoma: A contagious disease affecting the outer structures of the eye. It is only seen in developing countries and can lead to visual impairment.

Trade Union: An organisation of workers which tries to improve their pay and conditions.

Umbrella organisation: A large organisation which comprises and represents many smaller organisations which all have similar aims.

Visual field: The distance people can see to the front and to the sides. A visual field defect refers to gaps in the visual field. A central field defect means the person only sees around the edges of the visual field and has peripheral vision. An outer field defect means that the person can only see in the centre of the visual field and has tunnel vision.

Visually impaired: A person is visually impaired if he or she has a condition which severely limits his or her eye sight, and is prevented from taking part in any aspect of life because of barriers within society. These include environment barriers (e.g. cluttered pavements), structural barriers (the way things are done) and attitudinal barriers (the way sighted people think and behave towards visually impaired people).

Useful Addresses

Organisations of and for visually impaired people

Action for Blind People
14-16 Verney Road
London SE16 3DZ
Tel. 0171-732 8771

Albino Fellowship
c/o Henry McDermott
16 Neward Crescent
Prestwick
Ayrshire KA9 2JB
Tel. 01292-470336

Association of Blind Asians
322 Upper Street
London N1 2XQ
Tel. 0171-226 1950

British Blind Sport
67 Albert Street
Rugby CV21 2SN
Tel. 01788-536142

British Council for Prevention of
Blindness
12 Harcourt Street
London W1H 1DS
Tel. 0171-724 3716

British Diabetic Association
10 Queen Anne Street
London W1M 0BD
Tel. 0171-323 1531

British Paralympic Association
Delta Point
35 Wellesley Road
Croydon
Surrey CR9 2YZ
Tel. 0181-666 4556

British Retinitis Pigmentosa Society
PO Box 350
Buckingham MK18 5EL
Tel. 01280-860363

Diabetic Retinopathy Group (A visual
support network)
Jude Andrews
7 Shore Close Hampton
Middlesex TW12 3XS
Tel. 0181-941 5821

The Guide Dogs for the Blind Association
Hillfields
Burghfield
Reading
Berkshire RG7 3YG
Tel. 01734-835555

International Glaucoma Association
c/o Mrs Wright
Kings College Hospital
Denmark Hill
London SE5 9RS
Tel. 0171-737 3265

Macular Disease Society
PO Box 247
Haywards Heath
West Sussex
RH17 5FF
Tel. 0990-143573

Multiple Sclerosis Society
25 Effie Road
Fulham
London SW6 1EE
Tel. 0171-736 6267

National Deaf/Blind League
18 Rainbow Court
Paston Ridings
Peterborough PE4 7UP
Tel. 01733-573511

National Federation of the Blind
Unity House
Smyth Street
Westgate
Wakefield
West Yorkshire WF1 1ER
Tel. 01924-291313

National League of the Blind and
Disabled
2 Tenterden Road
London N17 8BE
Tel. 0181-808 6030

Nystagmus Action Group
43 Gordonbrock Road
London SE4 1JA
Tel. 0181-690 6679

Organisation of Blind African Caribbeans
24 Mayward House
Benhill Road
London SE5 7NA
Tel. 0171-703 3688

Partially Sighted Society
Queens Road
Doncaster
South Yorkshire DN1 2NX
Tel. 01302-323132

Retinoblastoma Society
c/o Academic Department of Paediatric
Oncology
St Bartholomew's Hospital
West Smithfield
London EC1A 7BE
Tel. 0171-600 3309

The Royal National Institute for the Blind
224 Great Portland Street
London W1N 6AA
Tel. 0171-388 1266
(A full list of addresses of overseas
organisations of and for visually impaired
people is available from this address.)

St. Dunstan's Caring for Men and Women
Blinded in the Services
PO Box 4XB
12-14 Harcourt Street
London W1A 4XB
Tel. 0171-723 5021

Sense (The National Association for Deaf/
Blind and Rubella Handicapped)
11-13 Clifton Terrace
Finsbury Park
London N4 3SR
Tel. 0171-272 7774

Sight Savers
British Commonwealth Society for the
Blind
Grosvenor House, Bolnore Road
Haywards Heath
West Sussex RH16 4BX
Tel. 01444-412424

Umbrella organisations of disabled people

The British Council of Disabled People
Litchurch Plaza, Litchurch Lane
Derby DE24 8AA
Tel. 01332-295551

Disabled People's International
101-107 Evergreen Place
Winnipeg, Manitoba
Canada R3L 2T3
Tel. 00-1-204-287 8175

References

Chan, J.W. (1994) 'Visual Impairment in China' *The New Beacon*, 78, 917, pp12-14

Coleridge P. (1993) *Disability, Liberation and Development*. Oxfam, UK and Ireland.

Hull, J. (1990) *Touching the Rock: an Experience of Blindness*. Arrow Books, London.

Keith, L. (1994) *Mustn't Grumble: Writing by Disabled Women*. The Women's Press, London.

Mehta, V. (1982) *Vedi*. Pan Books, London.

O'Keefe, S. (Ed) (1992) *Living Proof*. RNIB, London.

Saxton, M. and Howe, F. (Eds) (1988) *With Wings*. Virago Press, London.

Further reading

Cronin, P. (1992) *A blind student in the regular primary classroom: methods of teaching*. Royal Victorian Institute for the Blind, (RVIB) Australia

Dawkins, J and Fetton, E (1990) *With support – integrating VI children in the secondary classroom*. RNIB Video

Fetton, E; Hampson, M. and Chovil, C. (1991) *Eye to Eye: tape slide package – understanding visual impairment*. RNIB

Fullwood, D and Cronin, P. (1989) *Facing the crowd*. RVIB, Australia

Gale, G. and Cronin, P. (1990) *A blind child in my classroom*. RVIB, Australia

Harrison, F. and Crow, M. (1993) *Living and learning with blind children*. International Book Distributers

Ighe, S. (1993) *What you see and what you do not see*. RNIB

Lash, J. (1980) *Helen and teacher*. American Foundation for the Blind

McKenzie, R. (1990) *And as you can see*. RVIB, Australia

Miller, O. (1996) *Supporting children with visual impairment in mainstream schools*. The Questions Publishing Company Ltd

Pfisterer, U. (1983) *Games for all of us*. RVIB, Australia

These books are available through the RNIB Book Sales Service, Garrow House, 190 Kensal Road, London W10 5BT Tel. 0181-968 8600 Fax. 0181-960 3593

Index